Teaching and understanding drama

Norman Stephenson and Denis Vincent

NFER Publishing Company

Published by the NFER Publishing Company Ltd.
Book Division, 2 Jennings Buildings, Thames Avenue
Windsor, Berks. SL4 1QS
Registered Office: The Mere, Upton Park, Slough, Berks. SL1 2DQ
First published 1975

85633 073 6

Typeset by Jubal Multiwrite, 66 Loampit Vale, London SE13 7SN
Printed in Great Britain by
John Gardner (Printers) Ltd., Hawthorne Road, Bootle, Merseyside L20 6JX
Distributed in the USA by Humanities Press Inc.,
Hillary House-Fernhill House, Atlantic Highlands,
New Jersey 07716 USA

CONTENTS

FOREWORD

This book had its origins in the International Conference on Teaching and Learning English held at York University in 1971 under the chairmanship of Professor James Britton. I was chairman, with Esme Crampton of the University of Toronto and James Hoetker then of the University of Illinois as co-chairmen, of the Commission which worked on the place of drama in the teaching and learning of English. Most of the contributors to this book were members of the Commission but there were some fifty others involved, from Canada, Australia and the United States as well as the United Kingdom. I am deeply grateful to all of them for the work they did during the conference which for all of us was both sociable and intellectually stimulating. Without them this book could not have been. This book is presented in two parts. Both parts have something to say about what it means to use drama in education. Part I deals with what we need to understand if we are to teach drama; Part II further develops this understanding showing how it influences the way drama can be evaluated and researched.

Norman Stephenson

PART ONE

INTRODUCTION

Norman Stephenson

There is a growing awareness among teachers that drama is a means to learning of different kinds. It is seen not simply as the preserve of the drama specialist or a matter of the public performance of school plays but as an activity built into the context of the English or history lesson or as part of a humanities or social education curriculum. If this interest is to be translated into action then more teachers need to be persuaded both of its usefulness and of their competence to handle it in their classrooms. Two approaches seem to be necessary, one experimental, the other cognitive. The first necessity is simply for teachers to *experience* drama for themselves, to be prepared to launch themselves into the uncertainties of improvisation and to take part in kinds of play which for many of us were long ago put off with other (apparently) childish things. Whether during teacher training or on in-service courses, even for quite a short period, immersion in some kind of drama workshop, involving improvisation, movement, dance, encounter groups and so on, can give the teacher not simply an idea of the techniques available but more importantly the confidence to allow his pupils space and time for drama. Secondly, on the cognitive side we need to *know* more about the way drama contributes to learning, how it relates to social or linguistic development, how it can help the learner to relate what is new to him to what is already known. There is a need for documentation of drama in action, together with analyses which will help others to improve their own practice and understanding. The chapters which follow will, it is hoped, contribute to this process.

To begin with, though, in this chapter I should like to consider in fairly general terms just what kind of activity drama is, since it differs in important ways from much of what happens in the school curriculum. First, drama is make-believe. It takes its place alongside those other basic human activities – story-telling, ritual, painting, music, dance – which involve some sort of symbolic representation of experience, the better to contemplate or savour or evaluate it. It is, to use the distinction drawn by James Britton in *Language and Learning* (Penguin, 1972) a 'spectator' rather than a 'participant' activity. While we are engaged in drama, whether as actors or audience, we are in some sense withdrawn from the press of practical ends. We are not required to participate in the business of everyday life, but can take satisfaction in looking on at our own or others' representation of the way things are, or have been, or might be. Total reality as we participate in it is often puzzling, painful or fragmentary and each of us needs opportunities, whether through drama or another art, to re-enact parts of it, to give them shape and relate them to our individual understanding of the world. The process of growing up and the school curriculum both offer a continuous succession of new experiences to children and adolescents, threatening to disturb the balance of the way they have pictured the world so far. Through a session of play or drama they may create a kind of finite reality, a temporary respite from the flow of primary experience and a chance to explore its implications and possibilities. Taking up a 'spectator role' in this way has a vital part to play in their learning.

The spectator role in this special sense is of course neither passive nor unengaged. On the contrary, a normal characteristic of dramatic activity is an active involvement in the representations made, whether in the spontaneous play of young children or in the public performance of older students. Involvement may range from apparently total absorption to very ready transitions from play-acting to reality and back again. Children particularly seem able to step in and out of their roles with extraordinary facility, sometimes, without even disturbing their imaginative flow. In any case, there is often a high degree of commitment to drama which is all too rarely found in other areas or activities in the school curriculum. An interesting question for all teachers is whether this commitment can be maintained when drama is linked to other learning tasks.

Of all the expressive arts, drama is nearest in its representation of experience to life as it is. It is the least abstract mode of representation – made up not simply of sounds (like music), nor colour and shapes (like painting), nor words (like literature), but of all the elements which characterize human behaviour: bodily presence, movement and gesture, role-taking and relationships, language, a physical environment. It is this 'concreteness' perhaps, this involvement of the whole person, which makes drama a medium of expression so readily available to most children and adolescents. By contrast, the operation of language, in reading for instance, is a relatively abstract activity. Furthermore, drama in the form of play comes very early in human development – young children accompany all they do with a spontaneous flow of dramatic play, mirroring or reshaping their actual experience. The fluency and delight of this play are perhaps recalled by older children and adolescents – the memory contributing to their enjoyment of drama. The normal equivalent of play for the young adolescent is often either day-dreaming or the kind of group fantasy which easily erupts into destructiveness or violence. Much gang activity at this age is a kind of play-acting, spilling over into the real world. It is all the more important, therefore, that drama should have a place in the secondary school. It may, first, offer a welcome 'regression' to a more active, pleasurable and sociable mode of learning than the often formal and individual demands of much of the curriculum. And secondly, with the knowledgeable help of the teacher, the adolescent may recapture something of the purposeful delight of his earlier explorations of experience. It may be particularly helpful to the slower learning child or to the verbally inarticulate adolescent. It is of course true that not all adolescents enjoy drama when it is first presented to them. The self-doubts and confusions of adolescence may interfere with the self-forgetfulness which is essential to enjoyment. Yet by the same token, it has a specific value and provided there is continuity and support, most older pupils can take part.

To turn from physical enactment to a consideration of process, drama is an aspect of that universal mental activity which involves us in projecting images that recall the past, elaborate on the present or look forward to the future. It is part of a gamut which runs from dreaming at one end to scientific prediction at the other. Children engaged in improvisation in an English lesson, for example, draw upon their past subjective experience as they grapple with the demands of a present situation. They may try out a variety of roles and rehearse, in realistic or fantasy terms, life-situations which have been or might be, including variations on the self they 'really' are. Through drama they give physical form to 'images' – half-formed ideas, feelings, attitudes – which might otherwise remain wholly private and unavailable for learning. It is a sense of this freedom which leads children so readily to incorporate taboo situations and language into their play-acting. Sometimes they are introduced simply because they are forbidden elsewhere in school and problems of relevance and control do arise. It is important though that as far as possible *all* the individual's experience is valued by his fellows and by the teacher as a potential contribution to the general task. It is a feature of improvisation that it enables pupils to incorporate elements of their own immediate situation into the imagined story or action. So, for example, what begins as the story of Theseus and the Minotaur may include elements of the relationships existing among the group engaged in the improvisation, as well as the enactment of the private fears or aspirations of some of them. In the same way, a topic drawn from history of social studies may be taken up and developed by a group in terms of their own needs and feelings. Dramatic play may enable them to engage imaginatively with items of information which otherwise remain inert and unassimilated. Fantasy and feeling accompany all learning and in drama are explicitly sanctioned. This is of value for all pupils, and particularly perhaps for those who feel alienated from the school and its curriculum, since all too often they feel *their* experience is irrelevant to the school's purposes.

Drama is a social activity. Young children may play by themselves – though they learn to do so from their mothers or other children – and older people may rehearse imaginary situations in the privacy of their own heads, but essentially drama happens in groups. This means that the representation of experience which each individual offers to the group is subject to the scrutiny of the rest. Whether in the discussion that often precedes or follows (or even accompanies) an improvisation or in the action itself, the 'versions' which each participant offers are, or may be, modified by those of others, who in turn must modify their own. It is as though each individual fantasy is subjected to a kind of 'reality-test' – something which does not happen, for instance, in day-dreaming. The precise patterns of these modifications may be very complex. Sometimes it may happen that one individual uses the other, more or less willing, members of the group to play out his own representation of experience. At other times one may start the group off, but give way to others as the action progresses. And sometimes the improvisation may be inextricably a group creation. The opportunities for social learning are evident, and more readily accepted perhaps because the activity is a 'make-believe' one. A pupil who may be having difficulties in his real social relationships may welcome the relief of playing at being someone else, for example, or himself in an imaginary situation. The demands of reality often bear down heavily upon the older child or adolescent and he may be reluctant to take risks in his learning, social or otherwise. Drama is one of the ways in which his initiative and creative playfulness can be sustained and encouraged to develop.

In the context of school, drama is normally accompanied by a flow of talk – planning, taking decisions, analysing success or failure. Sometimes an issue that has been presented in dramatic form or an impasse that has been reached in a particular piece of drama will erupt into real talk about real issues. It may be about *how* a situation or character should be presented dramatically or it may concern *what* the truth or morality of a dramatic representation is. The possibilities for learning are evident. Talking and improvisations are both social activities, with the individual's efforts to express himself supported and extended by others. This may be one reason why both come relatively easily to most children, provided only that the terms of their contributions are accepted by the teacher and others unconditionally. When confidence and fluency are established, not only are talk and drama fulfilling their function in the pupils' development but they are laying the ground for those other more solitary activities which form a large part of the curriculum – reading and writing. For these are 'monologue' rather than 'dialogue', having to be sustained by the individual without the continuous presence and support of others,[1] and for that reason, perhaps, particularly difficult for many children and adolescents. Such solitary skills are essential to learning, but it may be that many pupils need considerable and continuous experience of dialogue forms to acquire and extend them. Talking about and improvising on a topic in history or social studies, for example, my help pupils to read with greater understanding and to write with fuller commitment.

The role of the teacher in drama is a critical one. He has to set up some kind of structure, however informal, which will at the same time encourage pupils' spontaneity and engage them in purposeful learning. In an important sense he is dependent on them for the contribution they make, for it is on this he works in collaboration with them. He has no set body of knowledge to impart, or even a range of skills to be taught – rather he sets in train a process

[1] See: J Moffatt, (1968) *Teaching the Universe of Discourse*, Boston: Houghton Mifflin.

whose end he cannot know. It is this element of risk, both for the teacher and his pupils, which is at once a necessary condition of improvisation and a source of uncertainty. For both there may be anxiety lest the energy released by dramatic play lead to loss of control or the demands made by the unexpected prove too great. The teacher's fears on this score are easily understood. His reputation among his colleagues as a competent teacher may be at risk. If the demands made by pupils upon his resourcefulness and stamina prove too great, his own self-confidence may be threatened. To have a reasonable chance of success, teachers who make use of drama in their lessons need the continuous backing and understanding of colleagues and head. It is perhaps less obvious that children's 'misbehaviour' in the context of drama is not always simple mischievousness or an expression of delight in the lifting of normal restraints. It can be an expression of anxiety, a nervous refusal to engage with the exacting demands of improvisation. An important aspect of the teacher's role is to provide the support which his pupils may need and to give them the confidence that they can be successful. He has to keep a delicate balance between providing the freedom to experiment and sufficient structure to ensure as far as possible that the experience is a satisfying one for them. Overmuch direction and he simply becomes a puppet-master stifling initiative and spontaneity; too little, and nothing in the way of constructive learning can take place. He has to be flexible, sometimes encouraging, sometimes challenging or feeding in new ideas or information, always receptive to what his pupils are offering. He is himself a factor in the situation and has to be ready to open himself to his pupils. He may on occasion take a role in the action, perhaps lifting the level of awareness or response. At all times he has to preserve for himself and his pupils a clear view of what his objectives are in terms of their learning. These may be of two kinds, operating simultaneously. First, they may be 'instrumental' – for example, an English teacher may be using improvisation as a means, say, to a better understanding of the language and exercise of authority or a history teacher to an awareness of the nature of historical evidence. And secondly, they may be in terms of pupils' growing capacity to do drama itself. The first kind of objective is perhaps more easily stated and assessed than the second, for development in drama is not easily described. It does not follow a straightforward sequential model, for the youngest children are generally highly competent play-actors. It is by no means certain that exposure to 'theatre' will be helpful, whether by seeing professional actors at work or by staging public performances. It is not so much a question of learning better techniques as of an increase in the level of complexity of the matters dealt with through drama – the feelings, the ideas, the relationships represented and managed. In this perhaps there is an analogy with language development: the techniques are acquired but they are best not taught separately from their use. There may too be development along the social dimension of drama – with experience and maturation pupils will become more aware of others in the dramatic situation. The capacity to respond appropriately, both verbally and non-verbally, to the other players in the action might be expected to increase and to be accompanied by a growing confidence in the ability to handle the unexpected.

The claims made for drama by enthusiasts are often exaggerated and always difficult to substantiate. Yet its potential as a mode of learning is evident and increasingly recognized. Many more teachers would incorporate it into their teaching if they were better informed about exactly how it could contribute to their pupils' learning. There is a need for more detailed descriptions and analyses of drama at work in the classroom. Teachers themselves are in the best position to provide them.

CHAPTER 1.

EXPERIENCING DRAMA

Nick Otty

'They are playing a game. They are playing at not playing a game. If I show them I see they are, I shall break the rules and they will punish me. I must play their game, of not seeing I see the game.'

R.D. Laing,
from *Knots*

Although the 'movement' session was not the first item on the programme of the York International Conference on the Teaching and Learning of English, 1971, my memory of the drama commission is that it really got started when Bill Tindall said, to an orderly circle of rather solemn intellectuals: 'Choose a partner. Place your hands on his shoulders and his hands on yours. Now try to push him across the room.'

The circle fragmented into a number of grunting and giggling rugby scrums. Bill later told us how he had once been partnered in this exercise with a diminutive nun, who had pinned him to the wall in a trice.

'Now choose another partner, and again try to push him across the room – only this time use your buttocks.'

Again the results were surprising. Little wiry figures levered and twisted and jumped until great hulks lost their grip and slid heavily across the room. The laughter increased.

Later we slapped the floor with our bare feet, walking heavily with our toes turned in, and we leaped desperately on tip-toe as though the floor were too hot to touch. Later still we talked and argued and whirled and buzzed and clicked until in groups of six or seven we had filled the room with futile dadaist machinery. The laughter continued and now its quality was changed from embarrassment to enjoyment.

I would like to make it quite clear that I was, at that time, as embarrassed as the next introverted intellectual at the prospect (or retrospect) of group grope therapy. I was in fact much happier with the more usual conference framework we all know so well. I am thinking of the situation where the group hears a kind of lead lesson or stimulus, which will be followed by an 'exchange of ideas'. I had (and have since) sat on these occasions and looked around the group of faces, wondering who they are and what they hope will happen at this conference, while I waited for the shifting spotlight of the discussion to illume my own little area of the topic. I had often listened to and made those qualified and requalified opening gambits, seeking the group's approval for the present utterance, lest their incomprehension should exclude me from further participation. I had often found myself searching for the moment when I could make relevant the thing I had come to the conference to ask or say – hoping there would be a moment when someone wanted to hear it. And I had, (and have since – not only at conferences) often been helplessly aware in a discussion that the last twenty precious minutes have been spent by two protagonists peering at each other round a box-hedge of semantic confusion.

I do not wish to deny that there is often an 'exchange of ideas' on such occasions – between people who know each other sufficiently well to share meaning quickly – or when a quick turn in the discussion catches us with our guard lowered, and forces us to re-see what we have been saying or thinking. But the extraordinary thing about that movement session at York was that, without going at the communication-gap problem directly, it made us all more real to one another, and helped to make what we then *said* to one another part of a shared context of experience. The very simple fact of actually having been involved together in some of the behaviour about which we wished to communicate, facilitated that communication to an unexpected degree.

Other experiences carried the initial encounter between the commission members further. In smaller groups we worked at improvisation, or at a production of *Ars Longa Vita Brevis*, or made masks and tried to make a drama using them. And we also wrote (and not only discursively and analytically) about what we had been doing. Here is one of the poems:

> There was a moment this evening,
> Glasses steamed up, slipping off balance
> In one damp sock, while the air ripened
> In oaths and talc, the bathroom menaced.
> I thought of the same off balance moment of tension,
> This morning with the mask:
> "There is the bag, here are the materials . . ."
> What do I do?
> Innocent of all prejudice against this paper rubbish bag,
> It suddenly threatens me – challenges;
> "Make me" – "Who are you?" I mutter,
> Sourly wielding brush and scissors . . .
> Slowly a fraction of a face appears –
> Not what I expected; it's violent, twisted, sad.

A stranger and yet mine — or not really mine —
A phoenix rising from its pyre of copydex,
And spirals of tin foil, painted tissue and
Bewildered hands that snatch at glimpses of a personality,
Until a wave of glee sweeps me
To swift certainty:
Shall I ever learn to like being off-balance?

Francis Annett.

It seems to me to catch a great deal of what is different about doing and making (and thinking) as opposed to only talking (and thinking). It shows one way in which 'creating' can precipitate for us and allow us to profit from those off-balance moments in which we learn.

Off-balance from my own experience of the York conference, I began to think that the notion of an 'exchange of ideas' is a rather misleading one. At one level it suggests that we are purely rational creatures, that we listen with open minds to what people say, and that we will modify what we think and do in the light of reasonable arguments clearly put before us. At another level it makes me think of ideas as a kind of currency, and the seminar as a kind of stock market. 'A profitable exchange of views', we say, as though by a canny and conscious reinvestment of our mental capital we would find ourselves on the road to wisdom (= security? = wealth? how would one complete the image?). What it seems to me to ignore is that what we say, and do, and the capacity to listen to what others have to say, are all most strongly affected by what we deeply, and therefore only partly consciously, believe. (At this point I find myself reaching for metaphors from agriculture rather than high finance. These may be more attractive; they may also be equally misleading. In any case the fact that I find myself doing it, is an example of what I am trying to say.) The ideas we bring to (and hope to exchange at) a conference, are deeply rooted in our attitudes towards and beliefs about education, children and society. These in turn will be affected by what we believe in our guts to be true about human beings — whether, for example, we think they are fundamentally good — or fundamentally evil — or whether we don't entertain that kind of opposition. The ideas we express in discursive talk are embedded in a totality, a world-view, which gives them meaning. We cannot really share that meaning unless we in some way share the background. And we can't simply plant other ideas without accommodating them in our available subsoil — we may be trying to plant a calcifuge in chalk garden.

In fact I think that the accommodation of new ideas in the individual consciousness is more often a creative, imaginative achievement than a triumph of pure reason. We have not really internalized the notion that 'a body continues in a state of rest or of uniform motion in a straight line unless it is acted on by a force', until we have by an act of the imagination, annihilated all our commonsense experience of our universe. We have to reshape our memories of freewheeling on a bicycle, and of following an arching cricket ball with the eye. Even a new idea about spelling may suddenly reveal itself as being linked to our whole image of the teacher in the broadest social perspective[1]. Each new idea that we make our own will alter, if only minutely, the entire web of attitudes and beliefs which makes our consciousness.

I am suggesting that there is something about the experience of drama, (and of other kinds of 'working together') which can be independent of the *content* of the drama lesson, and which can help the communication of ideas by broadening, as it were, the band of frequencies on which the communication takes place. In order to fill out what I mean by that, I would ask the reader to think of the way in which drama is often deemed 'good for' difficult classes. Discussion of why this should be so has ranged from the theory that improvisation about a situation will have effects which will carry over into the real situation, to much more general claims about developing sensitivity or confidence.[2] The way I would describe some of my own experiences is that I have seen groups establish more real relationships with one another, and with the teacher, during, and, I think, because of, a series of drama sessions.

Set beside the experience of classroom drama that of being involved in the production of a school play or opera: There is a characteristic quality to the relationships which develop between pupil and pupil, and teacher and pupil, in rehearsal and back stage, which is utterly different, in my experience, from that which normally prevails in a school. Some of what goes on may be rather disturbing. Rows develop to a full flower they never attain in the classroom, but they are rarely closed by the simple authority of the teacher. ('Don't you talk to me like that or I'll put you in detention.') You find teachers *and* pupils concerned about lateness or absence, not on principle, but because such behaviour might threaten the success of a joint enterprise. (Why do so few school classrooms express the feeling of a joint enterprise?) One could elaborate this example quite a bit. The tension of the opening night enables more openness and communication between the member of staff on make-up and the cast than has been possible during years of teaching and learning. There is that rather sad elation on the last night which expresses regret that tomorrow we must return to tomorrow and tomorrow and tomorrow. There is, of course, a sense of occasion about the school play which is arguably not

[1] A far more eloquent example than these is Paolo Freire's way of teaching literacy by first liberating the political awareness of his pupils. See: *Cultural Action for Freedom*, Penguin, 1962.

[2] For an excellent account of some of the sense and nonsense written about educational drama, see David Clegg's article, 'The Dilemma of Drama in Education, *Theatre Quarterly*, Vol.III, No.9, Jan–March 1973.

possible on a day to day basis; but the quality of interdependent openness in the relationships seems to me to be a function of a certain kind of approach to a problem, rather than of the kind of problem being faced. And we might, I think, learn from that approach when we are considering more general problems of teaching and learning.

For example teachers have, in my experience, a tendency to characterize simply the groups with which they work. "2F is a difficult group," they say, "It would be quite different if it were not for the antagonism between Tracey and Liz." Or "My sixth-form group this year is so dull." I have also come across seminar groups who have supposedly worked together for two years, but who are locked into a pattern of behaviour which seems invariable. There are the talkers – two or three out of twenty, the semi-permanent absentees, the occasional violent-outbursters, and often a majority of cud-chewers or tremblers. And again colleagues will characterize these groups as 'good', 'bad', 'lively', or 'apathetic.' In all this talk there is a fundamental assumption that the group 'character' is either an unmodifiable given, or a moral problem evoking the response 'they ought to behave differently'. Similarly teachers are said to be 'good at leading seminars', or 'happier with a formal situation', almost as though *their* best method was best for teaching any content to any group. It is certainly often regarded as impertinent to suggest that teachers should try to become aware of how the sub-soil of their beliefs and attitudes affects the growth or atrophy of their relationships with their students.

Although, in institutions of teacher education, we hear much of the psychology of rats and monkeys, and of the developmental psychology of the individual child, we hear remarkably little of group (human) psychology, let alone the psychology of teachers. This is true in spite of the fact that in this society learning is seen as something which will take place in groups controlled or led by teachers. Yet significant work has been done in this field. Here is a sample, from Carl Rogers' consideration of the implications of client-centred therapy for education:

> 'So the first implication for education might well be that we permit the student, at any level, to be in real contact with the relevant problems of his existence, so that he perceives problems and issues which he wishes to resolve. I am quite aware that this implication, like the others I shall mention, runs sharply contrary to the current trends in our culture, but I shall comment on that later.
>
> I believe it would be quite clear from my description of therapy that an overall implication for education would be that the task of the teacher is to create a facilitating classroom climate in which significant learning can take place . . . . . .

> Learning will be facilitated, it would seem, if the teacher is congruent. This involves the teacher's being the person that he is, and being openly aware of the attitudes he holds. It means that he feels acceptant towards his own real feelings, thus he becomes a real person in the relationship with his students. He can be enthusiastic about subjects he likes, and bored by topics he does not like. He can be angry, but he can also be sensitive or sympathetic. Because he accepts his feelings as *his* feelings, he has no need to impose them on his students, or to insist that they feel the same way. He is a *person*, not a faceless embodiment of a curricular requirement, or a sterile pipe through which knowledge is passed from one generation to the next.
>
> I can think of only one bit of evidence which might support this view. As I think back over a number of teachers who have facilitated my own learning, it seems to me each one has had this quality of being a real person. I wonder if your memory is the same. If so, perhaps it is less important that a teacher cover the allotted amount of the curriculum, or use the most approved audio-visual devices, than that he be congruent, real, in his relation to his students.' (Rogers, 1967)

It might seem, by this stage, that I have moved a long way from the subject of this book, but I'm not so much concerned with drama and how to do it, as with how behaviour which some might label 'drama' can help us with the educational problems which Rogers implies. It may be that this chapter cannot really speak to you who are reading it simply because it is a chapter, flat on the page. I cannot really get you to share my meaning without somehow appealing to that context of shared experience to which Rogers refers: 'I wonder if your memory is the same.' All I can do now then, since we cannot work at the problem here, is to document some of the things that have happened in groups I have been teaching, which seem to me to show how the aspect of drama I have been trying to isolate (i.e. what it does to the relationships between those who are involved in it) bears on broad educational questions of how individuals interact in groups, and how one might work for 'a facilitating classroom climate in which significant learning can take place'.

Examples:

1) A disagreement emerges between two members of a post-graduate seminar on the teaching of English about whether or not it is ever right to hit a child. The protagonists have often argued this one before and they have a shrewd idea that they will never agree, but when the topic comes up they cannot resist a long verbal battle which is inclined to silence the rest of the group.

The discussion when this happens is very fluent, both people are very animated; it ought (one might idealistically think) be a real moment for learning. On one occasion I asked them if they thought they knew each other's arguments pretty well – they said they did – so I then asked if they would for a moment, swap identities, as it were, and continue the discussion, but maintaining the other person's point of view. The whole appearance of the pair now changed. The exchanges were much more thoughtful, less fluent. We all noticed how strongly they were tempted to parody their opponent's views when they had to utter them themselves. The exercise did not lead to an immediate point of agreement between the two, though they both said it helped them to hear the other arguments more clearly. And it also led to a very fruitful discussion amongst the whole group, about the value and meaning of argument . . . . the pressure to win . . . its use as a protector of one's own cherished views . . . and so on. No discursive talk could have achieved the same thing. The dramatic involvement of the two, and their presentation of the problem to the rest of the group in a kind of improvisation were the things that made possible what learning occurred in the group. (This is a technique which I first heard of as originating from Carl Rogers, though I have since heard it attributed to other people. I have used it, always with interesting results, with third year secondary children and upwards, but I have not yet tried it with younger children.)

2) Working with a group of first year student teachers, I sometimes suggest using 'movement', 'drama', or 'games' as a way of overcoming some of the constraints preventing communication. (The games I describe below originated, as far as I am concerned, from an 'interaction' weekend run by Ed Berman at Bristol University in 1970.) One involves the students sitting opposite each other in pairs and each trying to make his partner laugh without touching him. The members of each pair alternately adopt the roles of laughter-provoker or straight-faced observer. In the early stages of a group's knowledge of each other, it is fairly easy to get the partner to laugh, mainly, I think, because the game formalizes a desire, which most people have, to please other people, make them feel at ease, and so on. To go against that urge, to refuse to laugh, requires quite a lot of trust. The game has a kind of obverse version where one partner faces the wall, and the other tries to get him to turn round. This is much more difficult to achieve, for a number of reasons. Eye-contact is a very powerful communicator (a good way of avoiding laughter in the first game, is simply to avoid looking at your partner.) Also in this game the individuals usually band together, those facing the wall drawing solidarity from each other, those trying to persuade them devising various dramatic happenings in the hope of interesting their adversaries. On one occasion, when I was myself involved in the group of 'persuaders', I said, as the time was approaching for coffee-break, 'All right now, I think we should stop this game. Come and sit down, and we'll discuss

what's been happening.' None of those facing the wall moved because they could not know whether this was just a further ruse on our part to win the game. But at this stage two sets of rules appeared to be working in the group. There were the rules of the game, which said: 'Face the wall as long as you can'. And the rules of student-teacher relations – as internalized by these students – which said, 'Do as teacher says, i.e. stop facing the wall.' Indeed one student pointed out that the game rule might also be supported by the rule 'Do as teacher says' and that what had happened was that we were locked in a situation where 'teacher' was saying, "do this" and "don't do this," simultaneously. A lot of discussion of what the situation was really all about now took place amongst the persuaders, and it was all construed by the party facing the wall as more and more sophisticated arguments to get them to turn round. On this occasion the lock was so strong that I had to formally enact an infringement of the rules of the game, by turning each student round physically, in order to release them. I think this series of events points to a number of interesting ways of seeing drama and learning and groups.

At one level it could be regarded as an exercise in the effective use of dramatic technique. Can the persuaders behave in such a way that they will draw an audience even when that audience is determined not to look? At this level, it could be used in drama schools perhaps.

At another level it shows something about seminar situations. They are riddled with unspoken rules. Many of these may be good ones about listening to the others, or not all talking at once and so on, but if these rules remain as unconscious pressures, their destructive power may be (and often is) much greater than their power to liberate the communication between group members. This game actually puts people in a situation where the unspoken rules can be seen to be operating, and where they have to choose between conflicting ones.

Looked at another way, the situation provided useful data for thinking about the authority of the teacher in the classroom. As student teachers, this group might have seen that 'disobedience' or 'indiscipline' could occur, not because of a total absence of rules, but because of an unyielding conflict between two (or more) sets of rules. For example, in school, there are rules set up by the individual teacher's view of teacher-pupil relations. There will be a different set of rules provided by the peer group on the same matter. Then there will be the individual pupil's view, and the sometimes very inconsistent voice of the institution itself (we value each pupil as an individual, we insist on school uniform,) and so on. Some of these sets will be consonant, some dissonant. 'Unruly' behaviour is often very strongly rule-bound.

I don't know of any more effective way of opening up these ideas with a group of live people than by the kind of dramatic game I have described. I do know that you can *discuss* autonomy in a group without ever increasing the autonomy of the individuals in it.

3) Another of the games I introduce into seminar work is called 'Clay Pigeon'. The rules are very simple. One person stands in the centre of the room. Anyone in the group can then move him into any position, as though he were an artist's lay figure. Every third person to move the figure in the centre must join him there, so that gradually the 'sculpture' becomes a group of two, three, four, until all but one of the group are in the centre, when the game ends. This game is a very difficult one to document, because it is always so different in its atmosphere and results. It tends to follow the contours of a group's character very closely, and by expressing it, makes communication easier between group members. Perhaps one person will only intervene in the 'modelling' if he can provoke a laugh by his contribution. The result of this may be that the figures in the centre are left in extreme discomfort, and another person is impelled to adopt a more considerate position. Always, in my experience, the game is accompanied by reflective, almost unconscious talk about the 'meaning' of the moves people make, and this is one of the game's most interesting features, for people surprise themselves by the differences between what they feel impelled to do with the statue, and what they feel able to contribute to a normal discussion. It is a very involving game – try it. I suppose once again it could be used in drama schools as an exercise in the visual impact of groups of figures – and that element is, no doubt, important. But equally important is what it can tell members of a working group about what they think and feel about themselves and each other.

I do not offer this documentation as an adumbration of a method of teaching drama or anything else, but as a way of communicating an attitude of mind towards teaching. To confirm this, and also because drama teaching has always quite rightly sought to learn from the giants of the theatre itself, I would like to end this chapter with a quotation from Jerzy Grotowski. What he says seems to me to be applicable to 'the Drama', to 'drama' and, perhaps most of all for us, to teaching and learning.

> 'When one talks about a method, about the method of someone who was psychologically as shrewd as Stanislavsky was, as logical in his order of thinking as Brecht was, as technically precise as Meyerhold in his bio-mechanics, one usually wishes to find those miraculous keys which would exempt one from revealing oneself, from giving testimony, from the act. And when they talk about any method, 'my' method for instance, the problem boils down to the same thing: nearly always they see it in the categories of 'to know how to do'. When they say that Grotowski's method exists as a system, the implication is that it is a false method. If it is a system, and if I myself have pushed it in this direction, I have contributed to a misunderstanding; it follows that I made a mistake and one must not go along that road, because it instructs

'how to do', that is to say, it shows how to arm oneself.

We arm ourselves in order to conceal ourselves; sincerity begins where we are defenceless. Sincerity is not possible if we are hiding ourselves behind clothes, ideas, signs, production effects, intellectual concepts, gymnastics, noise, chaos. If a method has any sense at all it is as a way to disarmament, not as a technique. On the way to disarmament it is not possible to foresee any result in advance, to know what and how it will happen, because this depends exclusively on the existence of him who fulfills the deed. One cannot possibly foresee the forms we shall arrive at, "themes" to whose temptation we shall fall, facts which will follow next. For this will depend on everyone personally. There is no answer which should be taken as a formula to be adhered to.' (Grotowski, 1973).

REFERENCES

GROTOWSKI, J. (1973) 'Holiday. The day that is holy,' *Drama Review*, 17, 2, 1973.
ROGERS, C. (1967) *On Becoming a Person*. London: Constable.

CHAPTER 2

DRAMA AND LEARNING – IN SOCIAL STUDIES AND HISTORY

Gilbert Barrow, Norman Stephenson
and Ray Verrier

This chapter is in two parts. The first gives an account of a teaching project in the area of Social Studies, and the second describes a History project carried out in the top class of a primary school.

Drama as a means of learning, as a way of engaging children in different kinds of learning, is not restricted to the English lesson. Subject divisions are not appropriate in any case in the primary school; and in secondary schools a growing number of teachers see the 'concreteness' of drama as a way of helping children into the more abstract areas of the curriculum. Much of the material pupils are expected to work on in school – books, maps, formulae, pictures – already represents a relatively abstract processing of experience. By contrast, dramatic improvisations are concrete, nearer to primary experience and so perhaps more easily grasped.

INCIDENT IN ULSTER

Gilbert Barrow and Norman Stephenson

A group of six postgraduate student teachers, two with some experience in theatre, the rest with little or none, set out to discover something about improvisation, and at the same time to engage a group of children in learning through drama. In the summer of 1971 in collaboration with a local school they decided that their improvisation would centre on the then current situation in Northern Ireland and they hoped to involve the pupils imaginatively in some of the problems there. The group they were to work with were boys of 11-to 13-years and they took as their theme the concept of authority – 'soldiers *have* to obey orders; sons *have* to obey their fathers – or do they?'

In this section we shall be interested in two questions: first, how did the student teachers imagine and present their theme dramatically? and second, how did the pupils respond to their presentation, in improvisation and in narrative form? We shall keep in mind that one of the aims of the project was that the boys should increase their understanding of an actual political situation. It was quite a complex operation and we have documentation of only some of it.

It is perhaps worth recording first that the certificate in education course followed by the students, though it has a practical teaching element, was otherwise conducted in a fairly traditional academic way – with lectures, tutorials, seminars and an emphasis on *individual* written work. In this case six students voluntarily got together to explore through drama a matter of common concern, focused by their professional interest in children's learning. They worked as a group, without the direction or guidance of a tutor, having to resolve as they worked problems of leadership, of mutual responsibility and of carrying through the project over a period of several weeks. It is obvious enough that even so small a group will not find it easy to sustain their efforts consistently when there are so many demands on their time and when the work is not meshed into the normal (assessable) structure of a course. Although it was not possible to record the clashes of personality, rivalries and sheer administrative strains, they certainly existed and it is surely valuable for intending teachers to experience for themselves some of the problems they set to their pupils in this kind of project. One of them wrote:

> It has been something beyond our usual range of activity . . . . One of the most satisfying elements of working on this improvisation was that we worked as a group. We accepted each other's criticism – we all made suggestions about possible improvements, possible additions and so on. We experienced depression and elation together and this, I feel, is very valuable.

The Students' Improvisation

The students worked by discussing the issues and how they could be presented dramatically, and followed this by acting out in various ways the suggestions made. They drew upon their knowledge (derived from newspapers and television) of the situation in Northern Ireland, their insights into family tensions from their own personal experience, and their limited knowledge of dramatic form and dialogue. The fact that the improvisation, which at one level was for themselves, was also intended for final presentation to an audience of schoolboys will have affected its form – possibly in the direction of some over-simplification of issues. During the rehearsal period three full versions were developed (each was tape-recorded and transcribed, though the transcriptions were not used as a basis for the next version). Dialogue varied from one version to another, sometimes amplified, sometimes reduced, for reasons not always clear. Gradually a skeleton outline was agreed on, together with 'cue' lines or situations which helped the actors to make the transitions from one scene to the next performance.

The first scene involved a sergeant-major and two British soldiers. All the actors tried out the parts of the soldiers at one time or another but eventually two of them discovered that they worked well together in the parts so they took them on. The sergeant-major was played by one of the group with some experience of acting who was also an initiator in discussion. One of the themes which emerged during the early stages of discussion was how difficult it was in the civil war situation in Northern Ireland to know precisely who the enemy was, and this proved to be a dominant theme of the play which emerged. This first scene opens with a direct address to the audience, clearly aimed at involving the boys as quickly and dramatically as possible:

SCENE ONE

SERGEANT-MAJOR: Listen! We're in Northern Ireland now. We're fighting a war. It's your war. We don't want to be here, we'd rather be back with our wives and our families. We're professionals; we're paid to do a job and we're going to do it. We want your help. It's hard enough patrolling the streets; we don't want to be hissed at; we don't want to be stoned; we don't want to be shot at. We're protecting you and so please help us, because we're helping you. Right?
Squad! Squad, shun! You're a shambles, a disgrace to the uniform you're wearing. Shoddy. Talking. Slouching. You're on guard here – it's not a tea-party. Do you understand? You've got to be alert, not talking to each other, not playing cards. Listening and watching. You're watching for the enemy.

SOLDIER 2: Permission to speak, sir?

SERGEANT-MAJOR: Yes?

SOLDIER 2: Who's the enemy, sir?

SOLDIER 1: How do we recognize him, sir?

SERGEANT-MAJOR: Everybody's the enemy.

SOLDIER 1: They're not wearing uniforms, sir.

SERGEANT-MAJOR: No.

SOLDIER 2: How do we know who they are, sir?

SERGEANT-MAJOR: But they might be wearing uniform. They might be me. They might be in khaki. They might be any of these. They could be anybody, so you stop everybody who comes. You challenge them because they could be enemy. They aren't going to come up with a great big placard saying IRA, are they?

SOLDIER 2: No, sir.

SERGEANT-MAJOR: Is that quite understood?

SOLDIERS 1 & 2: Yes, sir.

SERGEANT-MAJOR: Right then, do a bit better than you have been doing up till now. Right, carry on. (*Exit*)

SOLDIER 1: It's all right for him, he hasn't got to stand out here. Enemy!

SOLDIER 2: Thank God he's gone.

SOLDIER 1: We can't challenge everyone.

SOLDIER 2: Have you met any of them?

SOLDIER 1: Enemy, they're not all enemy. He says everybody here is enemy. I mean, I know Irish . . . like that girl Maureen I met last Saturday. Right?

SOLDIER 2: Oh, her; you've told me about her, haven't you?

SOLDIER 1: She's Irish, Catholic, she's not enemy.

SOLDIER 2: She sounded quite nice, really.

SOLDIER 1: Nice bit of stuff, she is. She's not enemy. I'm not going to go round challenging her if she comes along. It's ridiculous!

SOLDIER 2: No. Anyway, let's relax a bit now he's gone. He won't be back for hours.

SOLDIER 1: Not this evening. Let's have a fag, eh? Five hours, eh?

SOLDIER 2: Thank God he's gone.

SOLDIER 1: He won't be back for a while anyway. Silly fool. I'm not looking forward to this.

SOLDIER 2: No. Cold, isn't it?

SOLDIER 1: Well, it's November, what do you expect?

(*Enter Sergeant-Major*)

SOLDIER 1 & 2: Wh-Who goes there?

SERGEANT-MAJOR: Come on. For God's sake. Smoking on duty as well.

SOLDIER 2: Never smokes on duty, sir.

SOLDIER 1: Never, sir.

SERGEANT-MAJOR: Never! Take a step backwards. Oh! just conveniently dropped by a passer-by and you happened to be standing on it? It's still red!

SOLDIER 1: We was watching, sir.

SOLDIER 2: Yes, watching everything.

SERGEANT-MAJOR: Take a step forward. Now listen. I've just about had enough of you two. You're an absolute disgrace. You've been told to guard this. I've been once and found you slouching and talking. You could be dead. This is the last time. What?

SOLDIER 2: We knows you're not the enemy, sir.

SERGEANT-MAJOR: You didn't even see me until I was a yard from you. Now listen! this is the last time I'll come back and warn you. If I find you again it'll be extra guard duty. You come off and then you'll be on for another six hours. You understand?

SOLDIERS 1 & 2: Yes, sir.

SERGEANT-MAJOR: Right. Is that quite clear?

The relationship between the sergeant-major and the soldiers is presented in fairly traditional terms, familiar from television comedy series and at times not particularly realistic. Sometimes the sergeant-major sounds more like an angry teacher: 'I've just about had enough of you two. You're an absolute disgrace . . . .' The fact that the actors were intending teachers and that they had an audience of schoolboys in mind may have influenced this. In any case, it raised in broad terms one of the facets of authority which the group wished to explore.

The second scene is set in the home of the girl Maureen, already mentioned by one of the soldiers, and revolves in part around the generation gap between parents and children – a theme no doubt of equal relevance to both students and boys.

SCENE TWO

FATHER: That was a very good meal, mother.

MOTHER: Glad to hear it, father, plain Irish fare.

FATHER: I deserve it, working as hard as I do – unlike some people I know.

SEAMUS: Yes, dad.

FATHER: You're a layabout, that's all you are, son.

SEAMUS: Yes, dad.

FATHER: Wasting time. You're not thinking of the future, are you?

SEAMUS: No, dad.

MOTHER: Listen to your father when he tells you some home truths.

SEAMUS: Why don't you leave me alone then? On, on, on, all the time.

FATHER: I have to, I have to try and keep this family going and I have to think of the future for this country as well, don't I?

SEAMUS: There is no future for this country.

FATHER: There's going to be a future if people like me can do something about it.

SEAMUS: I'm going to get out of here as soon as possible.

MOTHER: Don't you talk about your home country like that, my boy . . .

SEAMUS: Well, who'd stay in a dump like this if they had the chance?

MOTHER: Think of the upbringing you've had.

FATHER: The older generation is doing their best. We're making plans and we're organizing, and all the younger generation can do is just waste time, like 'er, Maureen.

MAUREEN: What's wrong with me then? What have I been doing?

FATHER: I've seen you, hanging around on street corners with those soldiers, those English soldiers.

MAUREEN: It's my business what I do. Anyway, soldiers are just the same as anybody else. What's wrong with soldiers? They don't want to be here.

MOTHER: Not for the likes of you, my girl. They're not for the likes of you.

SEAMUS: Oh, lay off, won't you?

FATHER: I'm trying to organize the future of Ireland, and what do you do, the younger generation? All you do is waste time.

SEAMUS: Trying to organize. You sit there and you plan night after night, what you're going to do in the future. When are you going to do something?

FATHER: Now you listen, son. I'm going to organize and I'm going to find some explosives and then we're going to strike.

SEAMUS: Oh yes, tomorrow and the day after, when are you .. . .

MOTHER: Don't encourage your father in his silly plans, he'll get us all into trouble . . .

FATHER: They're not silly plans. Something has got to be done.

SEAMUS: When are you going to do it, Dad? When are you actually going to get down to . . ..

FATHER: You wait and see. I'm not going to get any help from you. You waste so much time, you've got no thoughts in your head.

SEAMUS: Oh you make me sick. You just go on, on, on, complaining all the time. You don't actually do anything though, do you?

FATHER: You just wait and see. I'll get the explosives and then . . .

SEAMUS: Pah!

MAUREEN: Come on, Seamus, let's go out for a walk. I've had enough of this. No point in sitting round here egging him on.

SEAMUS: Look, Dad . . .

MOTHER: Don't you go near the soldiers, girl . . .

SEAMUS: . . .you make the bomb and I'll throw it.

FATHER: We'll see about that.

(*Exeunt Seamus and Maureen*)

At the beginning of this scene the father picks a quarrel with his son along lines which are clearly very familiar to both, as the opening economical exchanges suggest. An earlier version of this scene had been more verbose and less effective:

FATHER: Some of us not wasting time sitting round, drinking coffee all day long. Younger generation – who the hell do they think they are?

SON: Yes, dad. (etc.)

When the actors are not really imaginatively into their parts or into the situation, the dialogue of improvisation can easily become on the one hand halting or on the other, as here, over-explicit. Words may be used to cover embarrassment or may indicate that the situation has not been dramatically conceived.

Improvisation, particularly before an audience, is always a risky business. An actor may dry up or be thrown out of gear by another actor saying or doing something unexpected. Where a play in several scenes is to be presented before an audience, as in this case, there needs to be some agreement beforehand about when the scene shall end. The students agreed that, at what seemed to her an appropriate point, Maureen would break into the quarrel between father and son and take Seamus off for a walk. He would go off shouting, 'You make the bomb and I'll throw it'. The point at which she entered was different on each occasion and considerable tension built up between the actors at this moment of the play.

Performance to an audience introduces further tensions which may stimulate the actors to greater imaginative effort. When Seamus and Maureen go off, they meet the two soldiers of the first scene and after some talk Seamus in this third scene shares a bottle of Guinness with them. In earlier run-throughs the drinking had been mimed but on the final occasion before an audience the actors had a real bottle of Guinness. They were interrupted by the sergeant-major who once again shouted at them for dereliction of duty, this time including the charge of drinking. One of the soldiers still had the froth on his lips:

SERGEANT-MAJOR: And you've been drinking as well.

SOLDIER 2: No, sir. (*Desperately*) Frothing at the mouth, sir.

This was a genuine surprise element, certainly unplanned, and if they had performed again, it would never have been as effective as it was then. The sergeant-major was obviously thrown by this unexpected reply to his authoritative bark. He recovered well, but for the first and only time the soldiers were, just for a few seconds, one-up on the figure of authority. The audience loved it. And this added spice to the sergeant-major's next move: to inform the soldiers that they were to be given extra guard duty. In one of the earlier versions the exchange had gone:

SERGEANT-MAJOR: You're knocking off in ten minutes, aren't you?

SOLDIERS 1 & 2: Yes, sir.

SERGEANT-MAJOR: Well, I've got a bit of extra work for you.

SOLDIERS 1 & 2: Oh.

In the final version, after the unexpected effects of the Guinness drinking, the sequence was:

SERGEANT-MAJOR: . . . You're off duty in a few minutes, aren't you?

SOLDIER 1: Yes, sir.

SOLDIER 2: Ten minutes, sir.

SERGEANT-MAJOR: Bet you're looking forward to that, aren't you?

SOLDIERS 1 & 2: Yes, sir.

SOLDIER 1: It's been a long evening, sir, watching.

SOLDIER 2: (*In anticipation*) Lovely, sir.

SERGEANT-MAJOR: Well, I've got a little bit of a surprise for you. YOU'VE GOT SIX HOURS OF EXTRA DUTY WAITING FOR YOU!

The surprise of the unexpected impelled the three actors into a much more dramatic realization.

The fourth and final scene takes place again in the family to which Seamus returns:

SCENE FOUR

FATHER: Where the hell have you been?

SEAMUS: You still up then?

MOTHER: Doing nothing as usual, Seamus?

SEAMUS: Minding my own business.

FATHER: Ah . . you've got to mind Ireland's business, haven't you?

SEAMUS: You still planning, eh, Dad?

FATHER: We've been doing more than planning.

SEAMUS: You tell me about it.

FATHER: We've got something to use this time.

SEAMUS: Oh, yes?

MOTHER: Don't go on, Dad ... (the father reveals a bomb) ... Dad! Where did you get that?

FATHER: At last, we're going to do something constructive.

MOTHER: Don't touch it, Seamus, it might go off.

FATHER: Come along, Seamus, now's your chance. Now, you want to work for Ireland, don't you?

SEAMUS: Look, I'm not killing any soldiers.

MOTHER: Now he has gone off his head.

FATHER: You're not going to kill any soldiers, of course you aren't – just the Post Office down the road, that's all.

MOTHER: Don't listen to him ...

FATHER: There's no guards there ...

MOTHER: You'll get him killed ...

FATHER: Just blow up the Post Office. You remember that promise you made?

MOTHER: Put it down, Seamus.

FATHER: Do you remember that promise? You said if I produced the explosive, you'd use it.

MOTHER: Don't take any notice.

FATHER: Come along, Seamus.

MOTHER: He's gone off his head. Don't, Dad.

FATHER: You made a promise, Seamus. Come on, for Ireland.

MOTHER: Don't do it, for your mother's sake, don't do it.

FATHER: Seamus, come along, boy.

(*Exit Seamus with bomb*)

The actors had agreed beforehand that the scene would end when Seamus felt the pressures upon him to be overwhelming. There was a progression in the kinds of appeal made by the father during the course of the three versions:

First version – FATHER: Come along, son, you've made your promise . .
Son of mine . . .
You're not a man . . .

Second version – FATHER: Come on, son, for Ireland . . .
Seamus, are you a son of mine? . . .
Come along, Seamus.

Final version – FATHER: You remember that promise you made . . .
Come along, Seamus . . .
You made a promise, Seamus. Come on, for Ireland . . .
Seamus, come along, boy.

In the last version the appeals of filial loyalty, of commitment to a promise, and of politics all combine in the most powerful way. It is noticeable that the political issues are presented very sketchily – no doubt reflecting the limited interest of the students at that time in the politics of Northern Ireland.

The Pupils' Response and Follow-up

After the final presentation, which was greatly enjoyed by both actors and audience, the boys were invited to continue the improvisation themselves. They divided first into small groups and each group was joined by one of the student teachers. There was lively discussion of the play and of the issues it raised. It seemed that the 'concreteness' of the students' improvisation lent force to the boys' ability to discuss what might otherwise have been too abstract a topic. They had a particular situation from which to generalize.

After very little preparation the groups of boys presented their own improvisations which followed on in any way they chose from the end of the students' play. One group presented a scene in which Seamus throws the bomb and returns home with the soldiers close behind:

FATHER: It wasn't my fault! . . .

MAUREEN: You told him to throw the bomb.

SEAMUS: You were hounding me . . . Even if I hadn't blown it up, you would have been hounding me all the same . . . You just look for an opportunity to hound me.

For these boys the focus of concern is the relationship between father and son, with Seamus expressing what may have been very personally felt grievances – the Northern Ireland setting merely provides the background for the family situation. Another group developed a similar concern, though this time the son is killed:

MOTHER: I wonder what's happened to my son?

FATHER: Ah . . . I expect he's walked off. He was chicken-hearted from the start.

MOTHER: You shouldn't have given him the bomb. You shouldn't have given it to him. He might have got killed by . . . He might have got killed.

FATHER: He didn't. He walked out.

MOTHER: How do you know? There might have been . . . there might have been soldiers by the . . . by the Post Office.

FATHER: There's never anyone on guard at the Post Office.

MAUREEN: Trust him to go and . . .

FATHER: Argh . . . rubbish!

MOTHER: But he might have . .... might have got killed. The . . . the . . . How do you know there weren't any soldiers there?

FATHER: He's walked off.

MOTHER: He's only a boy.

(Loud knocking)

FATHER: Oh, I don't know. He just . . .

MAUREEN: He's doing what he's been told to do.

(More knocking)

FATHER: Damn soldiers!

MOTHER: Let him in, let him in.

FATHER: You do it yourself then!

MOTHER: I'll do it myself.

(*Enter sergeant with one soldier*)

SERGEANT: Er . . . You son has been killed.

MOTHER: Oh, no! Where?

SERGEANT: He was killed by throwing a . . .

MOTHER: I told you! I told you! He's been killed!

SOLDIER: . . . Gelignite.

FATHER: Nah . . . it's all towards the cause.

MOTHER: It wasn't . . . He's been killed.

SOLDIER: He killed my mate.

MOTHER: See, he killed his mate.

FATHER: Well, at least he's done some good.

MOTHER: That's nothing.

MAUREEN: He *hasn't* done any good.

FATHER: Well, he killed his mate.

MAUREEN: Should have done it yourself.

MOTHER: It's all your fault . . . You shouldn't have given him the bomb.

FATHER: Rubbish!

MOTHER: It's all your fault.

MAUREEN: What happened to . . . the other soldier?

SOLDIER: Well, your brother just staggered up to us and he just . . .he was about to chuck the bomb when I just had time to shoot him. He dropped it . . .

MOTHER: You see?

FATHER: Yes, he *dropped* it. He's no good, you see.

MOTHER: He's dead now.

FATHER: Huh!

MOTHER: It's all your fault.

FATHER: Well, at least he did some good . . .

MOTHER: He didn't do any good.

MAUREEN: You made him throw the bomb . . .

(End)

With the son dead it is the mother who takes his part and these boys develop the antagonism between father and mother which just emerged at the end of the student-teachers' version. They appear to have responded imaginatively, though, to the uncertainties of a civil war situation by having Seamus *drop* the bomb accidentally, at once justifying the father's attitude to him and mother's grief. The irresolution of the end of this particular improvisation seems very apt and may be an indication that the dramatic method has contributed to the boys' grasp of political realities and of the human feelings which underpin them. A teacher interested particularly in the political aspects of the theme would have decisions to make about the methods he would use to further the boys' learning at this point.

The boys' English teacher did a variety of follow-up work after this session with the student-teachers. There was a debate, there was more drama and then the boys were given the opportunity individually to write some kind of narrative. By this stage they had been thoroughly immersed in the imagined situation – this is what one 13 year old boy wrote:

Ulster Incident
'Hey, don't do that, I'm your friend, remember?' screamed the soldier, suddenly realizing the man's intentions and looking at the crude oil bomb clutched in his hand.

The young man was trembling and his head was bowed. Suddenly he hurled the bomb and ran away into the darkness, not daring to look behind him. The post office was left in ruins. There was no sign of the soldiers. It was late when the young man returned home. His mother was sitting at the table, worriedly drinking coffee. At his arrival she jumped up and ran to him. He shrugged her off and sat down at the table, looking into space.

'Well?' she inquired, 'what happened, Seamus? Did you blow it up?'

'Yes,' he mumbled sullenly. 'The post office and two guards. Just for brave big Daddy.'

'Anyway, at least you're all right, that's all that matters to me. Your father's upstairs. Here he comes now.'

'Well, son, what happened?' said the father rushing in. 'Did you blow the place up then?'

'Yes, I did,' mumbled the boy bitterly. 'Two of my friends bought it too.'

'Well done! At last you've proved yourself. I got another plan lined up for you tomorrow.'

'Forget yourself. Those were friends of mine. Do your own dirty work.'

'I am the person who does the work, thinking them up. You just do the easy part. It takes nerve to make up my kind of plan – it's easy to carry them out.'

Suddenly Maureen burst into the room. Father rushed to her to tell her what he thought was very good news. Maureen was instantly worried for her soldier friend.

'Maureen, Maureen. Listen to the great news. The post office has been blown to bits and two soldiers besides.'

'Two soldiers! Seamus, they weren't . . .'

'No, they were not,' grunted Seamus.

'You . . . you're quite sure they're not the ones . . .'

'How am I expected to know? I couldn't have seen their faces, could I?'

'Yes, you could, by the light of the explosion. I know you're hiding something from me. Promise.'

'I don't promise anything.'

'Come on,' said Maureen, 'tell me the truth.'

'It was them,' said the boy slowly.

'Oh no, Seamus, how could you do such a terrible thing when you knew it was them – why, why?'

'It was all thanks to our big brave Daddy – he forced me to do it – nagged at me all the time till I got sick, utterly sick of it.'

'You ordered him to do it,' said Maureen hysterically, 'you, you . . .'

'Hey,' said father, 'Wait a minute. How did you get involved with two soldiers, two of our enemies, two of them?'

'They were friends,' said the boy, 'Good friends – and I killed them thanks to you.'

'You mean, you've been talking to our enemies – the people who are occupying our country – you traitors!'

'We liked them, anything wrong?' sneered the boy.

'And you ordered them to be killed,' cried Maureen.

'Why do you blame me,' said father, suddenly changing his attitude. 'I made the plan to blow up the post office, not two soldiers. It was his fault, not mine. He must have seen their faces and known who they were.'

'But you ordered him to do it,' cried Maureen. 'He did it because he was fed up with you telling him what to do.'

'Yes, all it was all day was: 'Come on son, prove yourself, make a future for Ireland.' Huh! There is no future for this country.'

There would be a damned future for this country if you young'uns would do something about it. I'm going somewhere where my ideas will be respected.'

'But don't go out now, there's a curfew – you might get shot,' said mother worriedly.

'Who cares what happens?' grunted father and went out.

Two shots rang out in the darkness. Shouts were heard, then died away.

For this writer the focus is once again upon the relationship between father and son and he also incorporates into his story the friendship of the young people with the 'enemy' soldiers. Group improvisation, as we have seen, has its strengths – several minds and bodies are working on a situation, no one person quite knows what will happen or be said next. This unpredictability may spark off quite unexpected intensity of insight and feeling. But there are times when the individual learner needs to engage in monologue rather than dialogue, to follow through an image or line of thought to his own satisfaction. At this point it becomes appropriate to write a poem or a story or some other kind of discursive prose. The author of *Ulster Incident* takes the opportunity to bring together a number of the feelings and issues dealt with in the improvisations and bring them to some kind of resolution of his own. In his version – and this no doubt reflects something of his individual approach – it is the father not the son who is killed. (It might be that a group would have been reluctant to contemplate this outcome.)

There is much that can only be very speculative in this project – even with much fuller documentation this would inevitably be so. There is no doubt that the group of students found it satisfying – in itself and as a contribution to their learning to be teachers. It was not always comfortable – as one wrote:

> 'I suspect one gets most out of the parts in which things are going badly, even if this is embarrassing to one as a performer. If the overall result is too flimsy, this is deeply depressing. Given some success, though, the sudden panic-stricken awareness of one's

inadequacies is, as they say, educative . . .'

Educative because, by voluntarily putting himself at risk, the improviser glimpses a gap in his own knowledge or skill or capacity to feel, and is in a social situation sufficiently supportive and at the same time challenging to be able to take an initiative towards closing it. This is one of the most effective ways perhaps in which improvisation can assist learning.

It seems likely, given the enthusiasm with which they undertook their improvisations and the quality of the samples we have, that some at least of the boys were similarly affected. The content of their improvisations and writing suggests that they took the opportunity to articulate, perhaps modify, some of their feelings about family quarrels and filial sentiments. More problematically, it may be that some moved through dramatic explorations to a more realized understanding of the human background to the political realities sometimes blandly presented in the news headlines. Whatever the case in this particular example, drama clearly has something of value to contribute to pupils' learning in the area of social studies.

THE HISTORY OF CHIEF DAVID

Ray Verrier

This is an account of a unit of work involving role-playing which I carried out with a class of 10-11 year olds in a primary school.[1] I was concerned with the teaching of history and in particular with the related notions of memory and historical time. I began by getting the children to recall memories of their own and to talk and write about them in different ways. Then we moved into the dramatic exploration of an imagined historical event. I wanted the children themselves to enact the role of historians. It was decided to 'create' an event in history rather than choosing a real historical event because I wanted pupils to experience and live through the significant event internally rather than study it from the outside.

The most effective way of creating from within was by employing role-play methods. For this lesson pupils worked in the school hall. They sat in a circle and were asked to imagine they were living at a time when most people knew nothing about writing skills. This suggested for the pupils the idea of living long ago. "At present we are sitting around a fire, each person is engaged in making something he will find useful for himself or for others." Pupils started to mime activities and were told they might talk to one another about their activity. After several minutes I asked the pupils to explain *why* they were doing that particular job at the moment. The mimed activity

[1] My thanks to the staff and pupils of Clanfield County Primary School, Hampshire.

showed clearly what was being done. As various pupils explained their activities two significant things happened:

a) Children developed their replies by accepting what previous speakers had said, and a group understanding began to develop. Gradually the whole group accepted a common group identity and belief.
b) Some answers pointed towards a significant event due to take place the following day.

From these replies everybody, including myself – I found myself taking up the role of visitor to the tribe – discovered that they were living in the early Iron Age and that the tribal leader had recently been killed whilst out hunting. Tomorrow a new leader would be chosen as a result of proving his physical skills and then he would ritually be made leader. Finally the event would be marked by a feast. The visitor to the tribe then pointed out that probably many preparations had to be made and therefore he would let people get on with their different tasks.

Pupils then created a ritual ceremony of leader-making and followed this by a feast. The visitor was present, sometimes observing, sometimes asking questions calling for explanation about present activity or future plans.

At the end of the afternoon the people of the tribe were asked how they thought they might mark this significant day in the history of their tribe. They started to explore the possibilities of paintings and oral accounts.

It is important to observe that the event these children chose to create is one in which a time of change is about to occur. The new leader may prove himself unworthy of real leadership, his tribe may enter a period of decline in which their enemies triumph over them so that they lose a distinct tribal identity. Alternatively the leader may initiate a period of glory and prosperity leading to conquest and 'empire-building'. Change is essentially what history is about. The pupils' drama had led them directly into the start of a particular instance of change in the history of the tribe.

The next stage of development in the work presented a problem. Change is a difficult thing to appreciate for people living through it. Essentially it requires the spectator role of historian, or of one looking at change from a distance. The pupils had enjoyed the drama. Could they now disengage from the role of tribal people and take up the new role of historians, by looking at their created event from a distance?

The following week the children were asked to imagine themselves as present-day historians looking back through time at the tribe, and in particular its new leader. They were asked if they thought the new leader proved himself to be a great man who initiated a period of fortune and success for his tribe or a weak and feckless man. All the children decided on the former. The boy chosen for the leader was popular with the class. They were then asked, as historians, to produce a history book of the new leader. They discussed the type of material the history book should contain and decided upon accounts of the deeds of the leader which illustrated his 'good' character. This information, they decided, would be drawn from cave paintings, oral traditions and archaeology. The finished book was to be called *The History of Chief David*. The work on the history book was completed during the ensuing week and the class teacher typed out the children's work. This was very valuable because the children were extremely proud of the finished professional-looking product.

The next stage of the work was dictated by two factors: the obvious pride of the children in their book, and the unanimous opinion of 'the historians' about the character of Chief David.

The professional historian is always interested when new sources of information come to light. He is also interested in reconsidering the verdicts of previous historians dealing with his special areas of interest. I therefore decided to challenge *The History of Chief David* by producing fresh evidence and an explanation of Chief David which contradicted the book. As documentary evidence would not be available as a primary source, the nature of the new evidence must be 'archaeological.'

The new 'evidence' was presented to the pupils in the form of photographs of finds uncovered below Chief David's palace. They included well-preserved skeletons of human bodies, the skulls of which were clearly damaged; a treasure hoard; and a piece of pottery of Chief David. Far from being a good man, David had murdered his enemies and buried them beneath his palace. The treasure hoard represented items taken from his people by a greedy, self-seeking leader. These findings and this explanation would invalidate the pupils' *History of Chief David* unless they could explain the fresh archaeological evidence in a different way.

The children worked in groups on the fresh evidence and finally offered the following explanations:

> 'These skeletons were of Chief David's warriors who all died in battle in similar fashion. Honoured dead of Chief David's tribe are always buried under the palace in order to be near the living leader of their tribe.'
>
> 'These skeletons belonged to witches who were ceremoniously killed by removing the brain and firmly buried under the stone floor of the palace.'
>
> 'The hoard of valuables belonging to the leader was hidden for safety in time of war or trouble. The palace was obviously the safest and best defended place for security.'

In the light of these statements the visiting historian decided to think again about his own explanation of the evidence!

In the course of their work so far, pupils had been challenged to behave and think in a manner which is analogous to that of the historian. The role-play about the tribe and the subsequent writing of *The History of Chief David* were vital to the belief and involvement of the children in the work that followed. They had created an object – the book – to defend, and this defence was carried out in the same mode as that used by a professional historian when defending his historical position. The range of language activities involved in this work is obvious: discussion, debate, small group social language, role-play and imaginative written work formed the types of language situation encountered by the children. Research work, in the usual sense, was not involved and for the next lesson it was decided that the children should become involved in the close scrutiny of written language, using *The History of Chief David* as a source. I started the next session by welcoming 'members of the Historical Association' to the meeting. A 'visiting professor' was introduced (the head of the college of education history department) who chose as his subject the recently produced *History of Chief David*. The 'Professor' challenged two particular stories about Chief David on the grounds of exaggeration. He explained to 'members of the Historical Association' how oral tradition tends to alter the shape of the original event. The two stories in the history book challenged by the Professor are quoted in full:

> 'Chief David was a strong man and generous with the food as it seems from the paintings in the cave. One day he killed a bear and fed it to the hungry people in the tribe.'
>
> 'Chief David was a strong man and when not strong enough he could be very clever. When there was a feast he shared his food on the ground. He was rather a kind Chief and most people were pleased that he was their chief man.'

The Professor used these two brief stories as examples of his doubts. What does the last sentence of the first story mean – 'and fed it to the hungry people'? In the second story, what does 'he could be very clever' mean? Clever in what sort of way? Surely these were examples of myth and exaggeration. Could the 'historians' present in the room *show* him what this meant? Pupils then divided up in order to:

a) elaborate the circumstances of the few brief works of the story
b) show that this is indeed a way in which one might expect people to behave

c) make an 'action' statement of their thinking.

The elaboration of the first story which pupils acted out showed the tribe at a time of famine. His people are exhausted and Chief David and a few men hunt and kill a bear. They return, but because of the weakness of his tribe David has to go around his tribe and actually feed each member of his tribe. This is what the brief written statement means.

The elaboration of the second story showed that David's cleverness was that of inventing a new type of trap for his hunters – a skill not of strength but of clever 'scientific' thinking.

For the final session of this unit of work the children were presented with a few badly damaged written documents produced after Chief David's death. By the time these documents came into existence people had learned to write. The documents were incomplete but they could suggest that Chief David's death was a welcome relief for this people. Could it be interpreted in any other way? This was the final challenge for the historians of Chief David. It involved another area of language study in which the focus was upon written words and the significance of words. Again it represents an aspect of the historian's work.

This description attempts to show how pupils took a fragment of written information and brought life and meaning and interpretation to it. One of the professional historian's tasks is that of taking perhaps a few verbal fragments and imbuing them with meaning and explanation. This is essentially the activity the pupils were carrying out.

It is then possible for young students to engage in an activity which is parallel and similar in nature and philosophy to that followed by professional historians. The difference lies not in the nature of the activity, but in the degree of abstraction possible for the level of development of the students. Children's activity must be developed in concrete terms that they can see and handle. The principal too for achieving this level of activity in the work described was through role-play methods. The ceremony of Chief David was active group role-play (improvisation), but throughout the rest of the work the children were identifying with the attitude of historians – they were taking on the role of historians. The teacher took on a role as well. Without the use of drama it would be impossible to experience this sort of historical experience from the inside – and it is from the inside that it has to be experienced.

The two pieces contrast both in their physical setting and in the intention behind them. The Northern Ireland episode illustrates the use of drama as a means of self-exploration as much as a medium for studying an event or situation. In the second place, the emphasis is upon exploring a situation and events in order to experience some of the problems of historical enquiry.

The actual language and style used to report the two sessions reinforces this distinction. It would, however, be an over-simplification to conclude that the one approach is 'child-centred' while the other is 'subject-centred'. The students and secondary pupils are not just involved in psychodrama, nor are the primary children just mechanically acting out an academic simulation game. To aim exclusively for one or the other would have been to make only a limited use of drama. In *both* situations, there was certainly imaginative involvement in the content of the work; in *both* there were experiences independent of the immediate and official content of the lesson.

The bare fact that there is a difference in bias is evident, but it would be hard to quantify the 'amount' of each type of function. The problems of evaluating drama in such 'how much?' terms is discussed in the second part of this book. But it must be left mainly to the reader to judge what the pupils in the first episode learned about objective conditions in Ulster, or what individual children in the work described by Ray Verrier were experiencing of – for example – being 'off balance' as Nick Otty described it in Chapter 1.

Even the most careful reading between the lines will not have completely dispelled the mystery surrounding what the participants in these two pieces of work were getting from drama. While it would be hard to dismiss either session as completely non-serious activities, it would be even harder to say what specific learning outcomes had been achieved. In Chapter 5 Jim Hoetker mentions some possible strategies for analysing the 'Chief David' work which might be employed by an independent researcher or evaluator.

Hopefully, by understanding and recognizing the possibilities demonstrated in the two examples, the teacher will be less over-awed by this mystery. It is as work which asks to be understood rather than as guides to teaching drama that these – and the examples of work which follow – should be read.

The problem of how to set about using drama in teaching should not be under-estimated. However, until he is alert to the possibilities such as those picked out above, the teacher will still be nagged by unease about the course and meaning of events even in the more smoothly running drama session. It is through understanding as much as knowing what to 'get them to do' that the essential confidence for using drama comes.

This point is pursued further in the two following chapters. In Pat Smyth's chapter, which comes next, we share more intimately some of this understanding by observing in detail the meaning of the language produced in improvisation. After that Roger Samay's chapter provides a more direct example of how drama is done *and* understood in an account of work given by a teacher who deals confidently with both the How? and Why? questions surrounding educational drama.

CHAPTER 3

LEARNING THROUGH THE LANGUAGE OF DRAMA: SOME QUESTIONS

Pat Smyth

The ideas about the relations between the language of drama and learning which are explored here arose from work done some years ago. They are inconclusive and they arise from but a small sample of material, yet they seem to me to be as fresh and exciting as ever. I offer them in the same spirits as that which inspired the work in the first place: as an invitation, a possible model for exploration over a wider field, as a tentative pointer towards a solution of some of the mysteries which surround the whole questions of drama in education.

Mysteries there are and they will remain insoluble while the claims that are made for the functions of drama in school remain unsubstantiated by close observation and analysis. While one task here will be to examine some of those more familiar claims by scrutinizing some language used by children in their classroom improvisations, we may try to discover something new as well.

The two samples came from a teacher of drama at a comprehensive school. They consist of two tape-recorded improvisations on the play *The Bird-catcher in Hell*.[1] Two parallel groups of twelve-year old pupils of mixed ability did this work. Their English teacher had read the play with them previously and they had done some writing about the story 'in any way they liked'.

The situation bristles with important questions right away: Why was the story chosen? How would the language of the children's written work relate to the language of their improvisations? These and others we will leave aside and narrow down the task to that of looking only at the words which I have transcribed from the tape-recordings.

[1] Arthur Waley (trans.) in David Holbrook (1962) (Ed.) *Thieves and Angels*, London: Cambridge University Press.

Kiyoyori, the Birdcatcher in Hell. Our Central Question.

In his notes the teacher does not explain his aims in asking his pupils to act the play in their own words, nor does he delineate his objectives – he offers us what he *did*! So, impertinent as it may seem, we will do this for ourselves. We will assume that he expected the children's play to be a re-shaping of the original which would contribute to their further understanding of it. This is our *first* stage, our *second* is to come to an agreed understanding of the original play amongst ourselves. Here is my own version of the story, influenced by discussion with my colleagues but very much my own for all that:

> Yama, the King of Hell orders his Demons to drive into Hell any sinners that come to the Meeting of the Ways. The Birdcatcher, Kiyoyori, arrives undecided which road to take. He chooses Heaven but is seized, protesting, by the demons who profess to be disgusted at the wickedness of his profession: that of killer of birds. They take their captive to Yama for his decision. Kiyoyori explains that he kills birds to sell to gentlemen as food for their falcons.
>
> Yama, seizing on the fact that because falcons are birds themselves, Kiyoyori can be said to be a mere assistant in the natural order, is prepared to free him.
>
> The players then recite the sequel in No style: Kiyoyori is ordered to demonstrate his art. He catches some birds, roasts them, and offers them to his captors. There is a greedy feast after which Yama sends the Birdcatcher, crowned, back to Earth to practise his craft for a further three years.

Here is the improvisation of 2L. The comments in brackets are my interpretations of extra noises and tones which convey action or feeling.

The Birdcatcher in Hell

TEACHER: *The Birdcatcher in Hell* by 2L.

YAMA: Right men, quiet!!!

DEMON: Right master. . .Let's find something to do.

YAMA: . . .erm . . .Men!. . .Ping!

DEMON: Yes?

YAMA: Erm. How are you getting on down by the river bank.

DEMON: Nothing down there sir, only dead fish.

YAMA: Oh. . . Can't you find any sinners? (*Exasperated*)

DEMON: No sir. . . There's none in sight. (*Certain complacency, implies that it is not his fault*).

YAMA: Well: You might as well bring back your men. Go and get them.

DEMON: Yes sir.

YAMA: Erm. Where's that group along the roadside?. . . .Ho!

DEMON: Yes sir.

YAMA: Erm. How's your group getting on?

DEMON: Not very well sir: We haven't seen anybody yet.

YAMA: (*sotto voce*) Oh gosh. . .Well I need somebody. It's been a bit boring just sitting here all day.

TEACHER: BUT UNKNOWN TO YAMA, ALONG THE ROAD ONE KIYOYORI, A BIRDCATCHER, IS WENDING HIS WHISTLING WAY.

KIYOYORI: (*Whistles a tune*) Ha! (*Satisfaction.*) Here I am in Hell, well, really not in Hell yet, . . . at the Six Ways. Where shall I go? To Heaven or to Hell or down to Clevedon? Heaven isn't/is/quite quite a while/quite so far away. Hell? Well a little bit closer, Clevedon just down there. But where shall I go? I don't know – I think I'll go to Heaven. I got nothing to worry about. (*Demons begin to make noises*). There's some demons around here. (*Demons increase their noises of snorting*). Mm . . . Many, many demons. About ooh! Thirteen?

TEACHER: HE'S MISTAKEN . . . THERE ARE TWENTY AND THEY'RE JUST ABOUT TO POUNCE!

DEMONS: Get him. (*Sounds of struggle*).

KIYOYORI: *(Panting and swallowing hard).* What do you think you're doing?

DEMON: Taking you to Yama.

KIYOYORI: Who's he?

DEMON: *(In ponderous tones).* THE KING OF HELL!

YAMA: I am me! . . . King Yama!

KIYOYORI: Are you? I haven't seen you before.

YAMA: I don't expect you have . . . I don't come down here for day trips.

KIYOYORI: *(Laughs nervously)* I'm on my way to Heaven.

YAMA: Heaven.

DEMON: Yes.

YAMA: Heaven? What's that place? We don't recall sending sinners to Heaven.

KIYOYORI: Who said I was a sinner?

YAMA: What's your trade?

KIYOYORI: Birdcatcher.

DEMONS: *(Chorus groan great disapproval in mixed voices).* To Hell with him!

KIYOYORI: Oh No! What've I done wrong?

YAMA: Where shall we send him?

DEMONS: HELL!

KIYOYORI: Hey! Wait a minute! What's wrong with blasted cat – bird catching? I give them to gentlemen to feed their falcons on.

YAMA: Oh . . . *(all demons seem slightly impressed)*

KIYOYORI: See. Really I'm not to blame. It's all these gentlemen who feed them to the falcons – isn't it?

YAMA: Suppose you're right *(reluctant).* I'll let you have . . one chance, bring me one and I will . . taste it.

KIYOYORI: Oh they're very delicious sir – you'll like them! Right then! Let's go. Over to the birdcatching – to the hunt! *(Noise of marching to the hunt).* Ssh! Ssh! Be quiet! Who do you think I am? *(Noises of birds whistling. Noise of bird being caught. Noise of wings fluttering).* Right then. Got 'em. Now to cook them. Roast them. You'll like these sir they're very tasty. Try one.

YAMA: *(Talks with his mouth full).* Very good. Mm. Very nice.

DEMONS: Let's have a bit. *(Great noises of enjoyable eating).*

KIYOYORI: Do you find them tasty?

DEMONS: Oy that's my bit! *(All quarrel).*

YAMA: Mm. I'll let you have one more chance. You may go back to Hea . . .to Earth. Back to the World for three years.

KIYOYORI: You must be kidding! How can I go back? I'm dead!

YAMA: I'll let you go back. Here, have a permit.

KIYOYORI: Thanks. Now I'm much obliged. I'll be on my way now.

YAMA: But remember: Three years and you'll be back.

KIYOYORI: Yes. I'll bring you lots of birds. *(Demons display signs of surprised gratitude).*

Examining the transcript, our *third* stage, then begins in the hope that we may discover something about the distinct and special functions of it as the language of drama. We know well enough the strengths of story-telling as a means of increasing our understanding of what we have experienced or read about. We recognize narrative as an act of representation embodying relationships between people and their exploits, as well as values and events that might have been or might be in the future. We are experienced in the other ways of talk, the learning for example that can take place through discussion which leads beyond the experience or the story to the general and the abstract.

The first thing to say about 2L's play is that it proceeds by its very nature into the future. There is no calling upon the actors to reflect upon what has gone before. When the story flags the teacher does not intervene to say as he might to a story-teller, 'Well now, what happened next?' But to participate in the action:

TEACHER: but unknown to Yama, along the road one Kiyoyori, a birdcatcher is wending his whistling way.

Moreover, while the forward movement of the players uses knowledge of the substance of the original play there is not a constant correcting and reforming of that substance against *itself* as narrative demands. Instead there seems to be a matching and a patterning of it against the stuff of past personal experience, often first-hand experience at that. In fact the No style of drama contains within it chunks of narrative which the children choose to ignore:

CHORUS: 'To the bird-hunt,' he cried.
And suddenly from the steep paths of the southern side of the Hill of Death.
Many birds came flying.

The boy playing the role of Yama offers us an example of the kind of patterning we suggest. When his minions fail to produce the expected sinner, King of Hell, for all his brave beginning, becomes a despondent school-boy:

YAMA: Oh gosh – well I need somebody, it's been a bit boring sitting here all day.

The language he uses, hitherto that of war games, classroom organization, the mass media or whatever, all sources of his knowledge of the words of power, becomes that of the here-and-now twelve-year-old at a loss. His personal experience of the way in which one has to behave in the role of despot is not adequate to support him through the unexpected difficulty of the delay in Kiyoyori's arrival, a delay moreover produced by demons who could very well prove unruly!

We see the children's own special way of shaping by improvisation again when we consider their attempts to deal with Yama's interpretation of Kiyoyori's excuse. They discover between them that the Birdcatcher is blameless, not for the reasons suggested in the original, but because he is seen to be the victim of 'the gentlemen'. His excuse is found in the same spirit as in the No play but it is one that is less complex and nearer the children's world: that of stories of Robin Hood or, more seriously, their own working-class estate between the cities and the docks where it may be legend that gentlemen from elsewhere use the less-privileged for their own ends!

While these two examples show some of the pupils' struggles in their re-discovery of the story it happens on other occasions that suddenly the time is right for a special kind of union between the imaginations of the children and the theme. Then something new is created: when Yama invents a riverbank and a roadside, when the spokesman for the demons makes the river seem dank and sinister by his discovery of the dead fish, when Kiyoyori makes his goodbye a cheery leavetaking, carrying Yama's substitute for a jewelled crown – his 'permit'. This is a 'true' representation in an exceptional sense. We should rather call it a 'transformation'.

No less interesting are those places where the original is improvised upon in a more or less faithful re-shaping. The interests lies again in the special quality afforded by the dramatic nature of the representation and its essential difference from narrative. In my brief telling of the story of the play on page 47 I invite you to join in a condemnation of the hypocrisy of Yama and his demons, and to share in my disgust at their enjoyment of the feast of slaughtered birds.

I chose the word 'seizing' to indicate Yama's eagerness to find an excuse to set the Birdcatcher free after a good feed, and the word 'greedy' similarly is the one to tell you something of the unpleasant and disgusting way in which they all behaved as they ate. For some readers the clues may have proved too slight and a 'better' telling of the story should have included more description, detail and explanation. The tricks of the story-teller, his ability to choose the apt phrase and his perfect elaboration of all the inferences are not required of the children here for their zesty enacting of this part of the story.

KIYOYORI: You'll like these sir, they're very tasty. Try one.
YAMA: *(Talks with his mouth full)* Very good. Mm. Very nice.
DEMONS: Let's have a bit. *(Great noises of enjoyable eating)*
KIYOYORI: Do you find them tasty?
DEMON: That's my bit! *(All quarrel)*

It is crucial to recall that the participants in this greedy feast are the same who a few moments before were expressing indignant shock at the wickedness of the Birdcatcher. Here the children are discovering fully the meaning of the *volte face*, commenting on the guilt and the grotesque hypocrisy by their re-creation of it.

What kind of mental processes can we tease out from this? Our comments suggest they might represent an early or basic stage of thinking: a level of intellectual activity that precedes those needed for narration. Even under the pressure of the public situation, the tape-recorder listening (and who knows what future audience), the teacher present and active, this improvisation seems at times to place the children in a tension between the world of their past, new inner experience and the new situation which is the original play.

The Second Transcript: Some Separate Issues

The overall relationship between language and learning must remain as a matter of central concern in the discussion of the functions of drama, but several issues do separate themselves out and so will take a look at these as they arise from the second improvisation on the theme of *The Birdcatcher in Hell*.

Transcript 2

TEACHER: *The Birdcatcher in Hell* by 2L.

YAMA: I am KING Yama . . hey find anything to do around here?

DEMONS: No – not much.

DEMONS: Send your men out and catch us some sinners.

YAMA: Yeah – not a soul in the place is there?

DEMONS: No.

YAMA: I get lonely without the crowds around. *(Claps hands).*

DEMONS: Yes master.

YAMA: Hey go and get/go down to the Six Ways and find me a sinner or two.

DEMONS: Yes.

YAMA: Take a few of the blokes with you.

DEMONS: I have just been asleep for a couple of hours. *(Protesting).*

YAMA: Get moving.

DEMONS: *(Groan discontentedly. Hiss and move off. Marching feet.)*

DEMON 3: Right. This'll do. Let's get behind a bush.

DEMON 2: Ow! I've sat on a thorn! Ants in my pants.

DEMON 4: Get your hand off my back.

DEMON 3: It isn't me.

DEMON 4: Well somebody's got their hand on my back. This is a bull field isn't it? *(Unintelligible . . then shush . . shush)*

TEACHER: Meanwhile along the road Kiyoyori, the famous Birdcatcher is wending his way.

KIYOYORI: Cor my legs aren't half tired. Ah, ah, I think I'll have a sit down.

DEMON 3: Keep your head down. Here he comes. He's sat down. He looks a wicked man.

KIYOYORI: I ain't got time to go to sleep have I? Better get some more birds. *(Shoots).* Oh that's a good 'un. *(Demons watch and comment on the birdcatcher's actions).*

DEMONS: He's killing the birds. What sort of birds though? There's another one. Let's get him – ah! *(They shout as they attack).*

DEMON 3: Take him to King Yama.

DEMON 2: Drag him.

DEMON 4: What's happening? Come on!

DEMON 2: Ain't he heavy?

DEMON 1: Shut up. Don't ask questions. Carry him to King Yama.

YAMA: I see you've got a few souls – a soul here.

DEMON 2: He looks like a sinner to me Master. Send him to Hell and be rid of him.

DEMON 4: King Yama. Bow before the King.

DEMON 2: Send him to Hell and be rid of him. At once.

KIYOYORI: What else?

YAMA: Now. You look big enough.

KIYOYORI: Look if you think I'm staying here chatting all over –

DEMON 1: Shut up.

YAMA: What did you say?

KIYOYORI: You heard.

DEMON 4: Be quiet or I'll feed you to the alligators.

KIYOYORI: . . . right.

YAMA: What was your job?

KIYOYORI: Birdcatcher.

DEMON 1: What sort of?

YAMA: Birdcatcher.

DEMON 1: That's real mean that is.

DEMON 4: Blondes, or feathers?

KIYOYORI: Feed 'em to falcons. *(Mumbled).*

YAMA: Feed them to your falcons eh? Ah, that'll make a bit of difference.

DEMONS: *(Whispered advice)* Ask him for some of the birds.

YAMA: What can you show for us?

KIYOYORI: Any bird you like.

YAMA: Well, here's a pole. Get . . . hand me a pole over there.

DEMON 1: Here you are . . . pole.

YAMA: Now go and catch a few. *(Tramping feet. Whistling. Great variety of bird imitations including owl. Noises of birds being shot and falling.)*

DEMONS: *(Whispered comments)* Blimey, Cor.

YAMA: Hey that's enough . . . . . . Bring the birds . . .Bring them here and I will . . .them.

DEMON 5: Cook 'em.

YAMA: Ah, cook 'em. Hey you.

KIYOYORI: Wait a minute, wait a minute.

DEMON 2: Defeather them. Taste that one.

YAMA: You cooked it. Give it to me.

DEMON 6: Hey let's have a bit over here.

DEMONS: Never had no breakfast. *(The group situation builds up the feeling that the birds are delicious to eat and everyone wants fair shares).* Wish we had three hundred. Get some more . . *(The group feeling solidifies into the expression of the direction to let Kiyoyori off).* Give him a chance.

YAMA: You can come back some time but first I will give you a ticket to stay in/on Earth for some more three years and then . . . and then you'll have to come back here and catch birds for us.

DEMON 2: Right. Here give us the permit Master . . . Have to sign. I'll sign it. Here's my pen.

YAMA: Thank you. I don't need it. Right, safeguard that.

KIYOYORI; Right Cheerio.

Improving the Capacity to Use Language

The explanation of the variations in the language of 2L's improvisation in terms of a struggle with the content of the plot of the original play and the motives of its characters is clearly related to one of the classic claims made for drama – that it provides increased opportunities for using language appropriate to new roles and situations.

A categorization of 2L's language into two different styles leads us in quite another direction. At first sight the interchange it almost wholly informal but when we look on carefully here and there we can discover the children using quite formal literary language:

DEMON 2: He looks like a sinner to me Master. Send him to Hell and be rid of him.
DEMON 4: King Yama. Bow before the King.
DEMON 2: Send him to Hell and be rid of him.

The second Demon is so taken with the sudden access of power that he feels in his newly-found phrase that he rolls it out for a second time: 'Send him to Hell and be rid of him.' Clearly he is capable of entering into the grandiloquence of scenes that involve kingly power, yet he and the other children improvise for the most part in a *deliberately* colloquial manner by which they involve one another in a great deal of fun. It is actually the second Demon who initiates the scene in the bushes (which is stopped by the teacher!):

DEMON 2: Ow! I've sat on a thorn: Ants in my pants!

All the comedians in this play are well in their parts. At one level we know that they are making fun of *themselves and their situation* (we're going to get a bit of fun out of what teacher has asked us to do), but on another they seem to be actually accepting seriously a challenge implicit in the language of their model. The No play in Waley's translation, though couched almost entirely in Heroic style, turns on itself now and then ever so slightly and uses a language much more down to earth. Thus it carries within itself an element of mockery of the behaviour of its characters. So it is that Kiyoyori within the same speech proceeds from:

without a pang
I have the world where I was wont to dwell,
The Temporal World.

to:
Why, here I am already at the meeting of the
Six Ways of Existence. I think on the whole
I'll go to Heaven.

It would be easy to describe or even to dismiss a large part of the language used by 2L as derivative from television, comedy or playground humour and to suggest that the boys had refused or proved incapable of accepting the challenge of the original play. However, it may be they are in fact using, as best they can at their age, some of the linguistic tricks of the sophisticated translator, in the role of author or 'spectator'. Their choice of language indicates their evaluation of the experience and in this they are assisted by linguistic clues in their model.

Thus we can give an extra dimension to the whole question of the position of drama in the field of English teaching. The language the children are using in this instance belongs essentially to the world of literature. The capacity of the class to operate at a certain level of objectivity, expressing a total and continuous attitude to their material opens up a whole set of new possibilities before them. One of the major concerns of the teacher of English is to engage his pupils constantly in experiences in reading that offer challenges through the implicit attitudes expressed by the author. We know how difficult it may prove for many pupils to make these attitudes explicit in order to understand them better and to convince the teacher of their understanding. Here in the re-presentation of the play we have all the proof we could ask for of 2L's grasp of their literary experience.

Drama and the Structure of Experience: Making Forms

2L's improvisation also gave us evidence of their children's concern for the overall shape of their story. The shape they give to it is very much their own, one which depends upon three crucial parts of the story which attract them most: catching a sinner, catching the birds and enjoying the feast. Yama's confrontation with Kiyoyori is kept to a minimum, deliberately so, for Demon 2 allows Yama to spend no more time on his decision to excuse the Birdcatcher than is absolutely necessary for the action to proceed:

YAMA: Feed them to falcons eh? Ah, that'll make a bit of difference.
DEMON 2: *(Whispered advice).* Ask him for some of the birds!

The pupils' concern for pushing their story into its shape leaves them no time to explore the feelings which attach to Yama's predicament but this may be a sacrifice worthwhile in the cause of the learning that is taking place in another direction. On occasions when teachers feel a sense of dissatisfaction with what their pupils are enacting, where the improvisation seems to be a ritualistic presentation of the action without any exploration of feeling or motive, it may be that the attention of the children is centred upon making these total forms. The difficulties of the operation mean that the context of feeling is assumed, lying hidden beneath linguistic utterances which are barely suggestive of that context.

Drama as a Means of Social Learning

The phrase 'social learning' here covers a complex set of developments which may occur when a group works successfully together: individuals paradoxically are enabled to become more themselves, members of the group find new roles, help and support may be given to other members who are discovered to be in need, collaborative efforts may be made towards the successful completion of a task.

Claims for drama's effectiveness in encouraging these developments, because it is by its nature a group activity, have been widely made. With regard to drama in the classroom however, they are often made with reference to activities which precede the actual improvisations, chiefly in preparatory discussion and planning work. Are we satisfied that such claims could be said to be justifiably made unless they are documented by study of the dynamics of groups actually engaged in drama at the time? Clearly many of the comments made in previous pages have a direct bearing upon this question but we cannot make any sort of detailed study. There were obvious clues to intriguing personal relationships being played-out, perhaps transformed within 2L's improvisation, most obviously in the jokes and smart repartee. We can trace the different tasks performed by individual characters and note the treatment of individuals and their responses, and we might identify moments when group collaboration reached a peak.

But there are serious omissions from our material which make any real progress with this task virtually impossible at a satisfactory level. We have no knowledge of the individual children in the class, their previous performances, themselves as persons, nor do we really know actually how many children comprised the group. We need such information, which could only be supplied by the class teacher in order to make observations in full. For example, we could plot the role of Yama in 2L's play to the point when he rounds off the action by his masterly dismissive speech 'You can come back sometime . . .', but we also want to know what the relationship is between his performance and his personal development as a member of the class.

What Needs to be Done?

The questions multiply but they are not diffuse. They turn each time towards that central issue of the relations between language, thinking and learning. In keeping this as our main concern we might find some clues towards the solution of one of the biggest mysteries of drama in the classroom: that of so-called 'free' drama. When pupils improvise unsupervised, more freely than in our two samples here, with a stimulus less structured, what is going on? It is this kind of drama that tends to make the teacher anxious about his aims. He cannot discern with any degree of certainty what his pupils are 'learning'; language may be at a minimum, ideas which do emerge are often alarming or disturbing in his sense of his own authority – he may be shocked. We might make some guesses: if we are right about the basic kind of mental activity that improvisation can bring into operation, it may be that some of the characteristics of the drama just described are evidence of thought processes on the verge of becoming social, long before they are ready for any kind of audience. The language may be close to what Vygotsky calls 'inner speech', reduced and brief, the barest representation of a wealth of meaning. Though apparently anti-social, such play-making may actually be pre-social in its content.

We can make some guesses – we need more evidence. Would the difficulties of obtaining it be insuperable? I am left thinking that the best instrument of all is the teacher with the small group, self-conscious, watching, noting and recording, and afterwards reflecting and commenting.

Discussions about learning abound with words like 'stages', 'development' and 'progress'. We use such words for convenience and they may be highly inadequate for the processes we wish to identify. It seems evident that the activities we have found here did not proceed at a linear fashion. Any combination of them could take place within one piece of improvisation. It is likely that traditional notions of 'progress' in drama have presented a somewhat over-simplified view and have helped to obscure its proper nature and its true functions. A much more continuous complex of relations between language learning and drama might emerge with further study.

The role of the teacher is interesting and puzzling too. In no other part of the curriculum can it provide such alarm; alarm at the sight of the experienced teacher who appears to subjugate his class through the power of their own imaginations as he makes them improvise, and alarm when the pupils subjugate the inexperienced in their turn! What is the nature of this power, its relationship to the workings of language and what should be its proper exercise? Where do we go from here?

CHAPTER 4

DRAMA IN ENGLISH

Roger Samways

'The Prodigal Son'

This is an account of some aspects of a piece of work done by a teacher in a new comprehensive school, with two second-year classes (age 12-13 years) of average and below average ability.

The Aims of This Work Were:

To give an immediate basis for work on story writing, enabling written expression to arise from living the action through drama.

To allow each child to create a version of the story for himself, drawing on the ideas of the whole group as they emerge from drama and discussion, and to write it down in book form.

To allow a maximum of self-expression, decision-making and self-criticism to flourish as part of the learning process.

To provide opportunities for some basic skills work on such aspects of English as paragraphs, direct or indirect speech, punctuation as well as on aspects of characterization.

I hope that readers will be particularly aware of the importance of the teacher's role in the kind of work outlined here. This includes the need to be constantly aware of the children's ideas and feedback and to use this, and the occasional need to enter into the dramatic activity in roles other than that of teacher, in order to give added impetus or to alter the direction if necessary.

Why this Story?

Myths, legends, the Bible, fairy and folk tales all provide a rich source for the English/Drama teacher who is interested in the raw material for more detailed or extended work on various aspects of story, both in relation to 'English' skills and to dramatic activity.

In the past I have, for instance, used such stories as 'Jason and the Argonauts', 'Theseus and the Minotaur', 'Noah' and the 'Exodus' theme as the basis for such work as I am about to outline of the parable of the Prodigal

Son. It is particularly important to stress that when working with such material I tend to focus on aspects of the story which lend themselves to deeper scrutiny, incidents which are often not fully treated (sometimes not treated at all) because of the often over-simplified style of such stories.

The parables of Jesus are ready-made material for the English Teacher, who is not necessarily interested in the moral teaching but who can see in the stories the raw material for more detailed and extended work on various aspects of the art of storytelling and story writing. (The reader might care to consider the story as it appears in the *New English Bible*.)

There is here an abundance of possibilities which any discerning teacher will readily see. The English teaching here described attempts to show what happened when a group of 30 children worked on aspects of this story for a period of some three or four weeks, during which a drama hall was available for at least 80 minutes per week and a further three 35 minute periods available in classrooms.

First of all the teacher describes how the topic was introduced to the groups and shows the kind of responses made by one group in particular. (This process used up a period of 35 or 40 minutes.)

Teacher	*Class*
Took class to drama hall for space availability. They grouped around and when settled, were asked to suggest reasons why a young person might suddenly leave home.	Plenty of ideas, thrown out in a fairly noisy and disorderly fashion, but sufficient for teacher to hear the following and to discuss them for a few moments with the person offering the idea: Nagging or cruel parents. Wants independence to plan own future. No friends at school, unhappy. Daughter – expecting baby – unmarried. Neglected by parents. Two young members of family, one more favoured than other. Leaving for new job, student etc.
Now, having elaborated on a few of these suggestions with the group contributing at random (and certainly not *all* listening) they were	

asked to choose one such situation and to select the crucial confrontation between son/daughter and parents and to act it.

They choose own groups.
Disperse rapidly around hall and act, regardless of noise and other groups.

The teacher observes this and after some ten to fifteen minutes, when it look as though most groups have acted something, he recalls the class and asks each group to be ready to show their group improvisation.

Some groups act out their various scenes: mostly consisting of rapid and often violent episodes with very little depth of perception. (All the situations suggested by class previously are used here.)

Back together as a class – because time is running out, the final question was asked: What kinds of people have you seen portrayed in these scenes?
(Teacher wonders how much of this reflects their home lives and relationships?)

They readily observe: cruel, hostile generally unpleasant people (who usually hit each other) and do not discuss things very much.

At this point the lesson ends and there are still some groups who have not acted their scenes in front of others. Do they mind?

One group definitely yes, the other no.

Teacher promises that next session will start with this group's acting.

Next time, the class see the remaining scene and the lesson proceeds as follows:

Teacher introduces, by reading, the story of the prodigal son, using the New English Bible translation. "Here is a similar situation, I wonder how it was when the lad left home? Anyone like to act it out?"

Volunteers readily available – three boys act fairly swift scene as follows: Brothers watching television, one chatting to other about being fed-up at home, wanting to get away. Decides to go and see father and ask for promised share of family money. This happens and after some argument the father gives in and promises a cheque in morning.

At this point the session is brought to a close and the group is asked to consider for next time, what happens when the lad leaves home, where does he go, what does he do, what people does he meet?

Each group reached this point fairly rapidly and then developed it in different directions from here. One of the main aims was to involve the whole class in story building, through improvised role-play, enabling each individual to write a complete version of the story. The aim was not to *act* the whole story; rather, it was to explore in some detail certain microcosms from the story. (One of the phrases ultimately chosen from the original parable version for such consideration was the idea of 'squandering' his money.)

Each group made him end up in a city. It is easy to imagine how they suggested he would squander his money: gambling, girl friends, cars, drinking, property were all suggested.

As far as the drama and its contribution is concerned the emphasis whenever role-play was used was on the kinds of people the lad would meet and how they were affected by the knowledge that he had a large sum of money.

What follows are:

1) Some examples of the dialogue from group improvisations as recorded at the first attempt.

2) An account of a moment in the drama of one group when things went wrong and needed teacher intervention. (A situation all too common when drama is used and one which highlights the need to appreciate a particular nature and methods of the dramatic process.)

The 'Prodigal Son' meets some girls in a bar at a hotel. (Paul is a 'Prodigal Son'.)

PAUL: Anyone like a drink?

GIRL 1: No thanks, just had one.

PAUL: Oh, what do you want then? What's it like around here?

GIRL 1:
GIRL 2: Alright.

PAUL: Well .... where's the nearest beach, or isn't there one?

GIRL 1: There ain't one .... you gotta go miles to get one.

PAUL: Stupid . . . . . Uh . . .

GIRL 2: You're new around here, aren't you?

PAUL: Yeh.

GIRL 2: What's your name?

PAUL: Paul

GIRL 3: How long have you been here?

PAUL: Oh, about almost a week now.

GIRL 2: How long are you staying?

PAUL: Oh, indefinitely.

GIRL 3: Where did you just come from?

PAUL: I come from Cornwall . . . . might think about going to America . . . . but I don't think I will 'cause it's nice around here, ain't it? Plenty of sun.

GIRL 2: More in America, ain't there?

PAUL: Yeh . . . .Nice club you got here, ain't it?

GIRL 1: Alright I suppose.

(The girls in this group are normally very reticent in class – hence rather limited oral contribution make 'Paul' work very hard.)

He talks with another group of girls in the same bar.

PAUL: Hello.

GIRL 1: Hello.

PAUL: Any of you want a drink?

GIRL 1: Uh . . . . . no thanks . . . . . . shall I tell your fortune?

PAUL: Well, if you like . . . .

GIRL 1: Oh go on, just for a laugh.

PAUL: Alright.

GIRL 2: Go on then.

GIRL 1: Eh . . . . . you're gonna have a long life, and you're gonna get married to a nice lady . . . . you're gonna have two kids . . . . .

GIRL 2: *(Giggles)* Go on Jo . . . .

GIRL 1; Um . . . . You're gonna live in a big house.

PAUL: I expect that'll be true.

GIRL 2: What's going to happen to him?

GIRL 1: Plenty of money.

GIRL 2: Why do you say you're going to have plenty of money and why do you think it's going to be true?

PAUL: I've just been left a fortune . . . . .

GIRL 2: Who by?

PAUL: My dad . . . . .

GIRL 2: Second thoughts, I will have that drink . . . . . give me the money.

PAUL: Alright wait a minute . . . .. .

GIRL 1: And I'll have one.

GIRL 2: What do you want?

GIRL 1: I'll have a gin and tonic please.

GIRL 2: What do you want?

GIRL 3: Oh, I'll just have gin and tonic as well.

GIRL 2: Do you want one?

PAUL: No thanks, don't drink.

GIRL 1: Um . . . . . you'll have plenty of money . . . . . you'll have a swimming pool in your garden . . . .

(Notice how Girl 1 stays in character in spite of a lapse in the direction of the previous lines of talk.)

PAUL: Probably have two.

GIRL 3: You'll have loads of friends.

PAUL: 'Spect I will with all the money I've got.
(Drinks arrive)

GIRL 2: What's your name?

PAUL: That's a very bright life, ain't it . . . . . Paul?

GIRL 2: Where are you staying?

PAUL: Oh . . . . . at the Crown Hotel.

GIRL 2: That's a nice place, isn't it?

GIRL 1: Yeh . . . . . lovely . . . . . how long have you been here?

PAUL: Eh . . . . . um . . . . . nearly a week now.

GIRL 1: What did you leave home for . . . . or *did* you?

PAUL: Yes, I left home 'cause I was fed up.

GIRL 2: How many people have you got in your family?

PAUL: Oh – there's only two of us.

GIRL 2: Who's that?

PAUL: Me and my brother.

GIRL 2: What about your mum . . . .

PAUL: Yeh . . . .

GIRL 2: and your dad.

PAUL: I got a mum and dad.

GIRL 1:
GIRL 2: What? How come?

GIRL 2: How come you come in a pub then to have a drink?

PAUL: . . . . just trying to pick up a few friends.

GIRL 2: Oh go on Joanne, finish telling his fortune off –

GIRL 1: I finished.

GIRL 2: You haven't.

GIRL 1: I have.

GIRL 2: Come on . . . .

GIRL 1: I have . . . . . I finished . . . . .

PAUL: What's your name?

PAT: Pat . . . . .

PAUL: What's yours?

GIRL 3: Bridgette.

PAUL: What's yours?

GIRL 2: Anita.

GIRL 1: Joanne.

PAUL: Joanne.

GIRL 1: What you think of doing for the rest of the time you're staying here?

PAUL: Well, I was thinking of going down to the beach – going to be a bit far so I'll have to buy myself a car.

GIRL 2: Whose is that white one out there?
(This was a white Rolls Royce!)

PAUL: Oh – I'll have to take him down the scrap heap – 'e's no good.

GIRL 2: He's alright.

PAUL: Well . . . . .

GIRL 2: What job have you got or ain't you got one yet?

PAUL: I don't need a job.

GIRL 2: Why – what if you run out of money?

PAUL: Just hard luck, ain't it.

GIRL 2: No – if you did ever get a job what sort of job have you in mind?

PAUL: Oh – probably start my own lorry firm – you know carriers and that.

GIRL 1: Lorries.

PAUL: Don't you like 'em?

GIRL 1: No – dangerous I reckon.

PAUL: No – if they're driven properly they're alright.

Both these pieces were recorded during a period of 80 minutes in which the whole class of 28 was involved in improvising a scene where the 'Prodigal Son' (Paul) went into a hotel club-bar having arrived in the city.

The only structure imposed by the teacher was that of ensuring that Paul went to each group in the room and that, for recording purposes, the others should be quiet while he talked with a group at a time.

This was in response to the simple question – where does he go and what does he do once he arrives in the City?

The other class made him go to a gambling club, a pub, a men's sports club and a hotel. In every case he was meeting *people* which was valuable material for the story and character descriptions in particular.

Another key question asked now, was what kinds of people does he meet who try to take advantage of his money? What follows is an example of a small group improvisation in response to this.

(This scene took place at the front of a fairly small classroom with the rest of the class sitting around listening.)

BOY 1: Hello Sir – we're here about racing cars – about stock-car racing – we come from Swindon.

PAUL: Right down there?

BOY 1: Yes – we've just come up here to look around for a few people – see if we could raise any money for 'em?

PAUL: What the stock-cars or the people?

BOY 1: Yeh – well for the stock-cars – see – go round asking people and all that lot – you know . . . .

BOY 2: . . . . if they'd like to join the club – cause eh . . we've got this club – and at the moment we've got 140 members – and – we'd like . . . . a few more – we come here to see if we could get a few more.

PAUL: Well, what do members do?

BOY 1: Oh well they . . . . we got a club up there – they go stock-car racing and racing – and after they've won they say like get about £50. Then they come back into the club and have a drink and all that.

PAUL: Well, what do you want . . . . exactly want me to do?

BOY 1: Well, we want you to come and join see . . See if you can put any money towards some cars.

PAUL: How much money?

BOY 1: Oh . . . about . . . have a look . . . where's your notebook . . . got the numbers?

BOY 2: Here's our member-card anyway . . . . You got the numbers?

BOY 1: Yes . . . . we need about £7,000.

PAUL: £7,000!

BOY 1: Not only from you . . yes . . but not only from you see . . . We just want to know how much you can put towards – you know £7,000.

PAUL: Well, I expect I can give about eh . . . £4,000.

BOY 1: Yes . . .that'll be alright won't it – that'll be very good – Sir.

PAUL: £4,000 . . . . I'll have to go to the bank . . . . where's the (Yeh) this club held?

BOY 1: Oh . . . down Swindon . . . in um . .

BOY 2: You go down . . . .

PAUL: What about the transport down to Swindon?

BOY 1: Oh we got our own transport.

PAUL: Yes – but what about me?

BOY 1: Yes, well we could pick you up. When would you like to go down . . . when would you like to . . .

PAUL: When's the club? When are they held?

BOY 1: Well they have them Mondays, Wednesdays, Thursdays and Saturdays.

PAUL: Well, tomorrow's Thursday . . . . if you like to come up and pick me up I'll have the money ready.

BOY 1: Yes . . . where will you be to?

PAUL: Well – up in my hotel up Park Street.

BOY 1: What time shall we pick you up?

BOY 2: Ten o'clock . . about that?

PAUL: Yes – about 10 o'clock – that'll do . . . O.K. *(exit Paul)*

BOY 2: Hey – that's alright then . . .

(Boy 2 of is particularly 'low ability' and it is interesting to note his reversion to more colloquial style here having maintained something more formal for quite a while.)

BOY 1: Yeh £4,000.

BOY 2: Made £1,000 out of that . . . .we only needed £3,000 really . . . .

BOY 1: Yeh.

BOY 2: – for those cars.

BOY 1: Have £1,000 for ourselves won't us?

BOY 2: Yeh. . . .

BOY 1: Not bad . . . .

BOY 2: Got 'ee well dun us?

BOY 1: Yeh.

Here – two boys were deliberately setting out to cheat Paul out of some money. Following this there was no lack of examples of other types of people who might take advantage of the situation – including a group of girls who were determined to charm him into parting with some to help them in setting up a hairdressing salon!

I hope these examples are sufficient to illustrate the variety and quantity of material that emerges as a result of the drama. It should be obvious enough how this can relate directly to work in English. The order is usually TALK, ACT, TALK, WRITE.

In case any readers should think that this kind of drama always works and produces neat end products that are easily taped and transcribed, here is an example of the drama session going badly wrong and where there was a definite need for teacher intervention and participation: A large group of boys from one of the classes decided that they would take advantage of Paul by ambushing his car on the motorway, beating him up and stealing his money there and then.

They carefully prepared the Hall with the portable wooden staging – blocks as cars, then proceeded to act out a motorway chase culminating in a sandwiching of Paul's car between two others. This was followed by a fight which left Paul staggering to a phone to ring the police. Within seconds the police (more boys) had arrived and together with Paul (now fit and well) had pursued the robbers to their hideout where a free-for-all fight developed. This went on for a few minutes becoming more and more chaotic, the boys enjoying the romp and the rest of the class wondering what 'sir' would do about it. With a firm clap of the hands and a loud shout from the teacher, the boys stopped their fighting and the whole group then discussed with the teacher 'what was wrong with that?' Those who had watched were particularly critical of the events immediately following the phone call. They could accept what happened before (with some dramatic licence), but not the subsequent chasing and falling about. Closer questioning revealed the criticism that 'the police wouldn't have behaved like that'. (The boys involved agreed with their critics!)

At this point the teacher decided that the focus should be on that 'phone call in order to illustrate the need for a more realistic and convincing portrayal of what might have happened, showing that the dramatic process does impose by its very nature a structure which is quite definite, involving 'total make-believe' and concerning details of importance in relation to the real action of the story, in this case what really happens when that phone call is made. So, the 'phone call was made again by Paul and the teacher lifted the receiver as the officer on duty at the station. He insisted on adequate details from the boy concerning time and place, descriptions of men, cars, etc., (none of which occurred before – it was more a matter of 'I've been beaten up and robbed – come quickly').

Thus, by entering in role as policeman, the teacher was able to give the drama a necessary boost and direct it along more profitable lines. He was able to lead into a discussion with the class as to whether drama was able to show everything that happened (or indeed, needed to). The children are inevitably influenced by film or T.V. so that 'doing' a cops and robbers chase seems to them to be easy.

The dramatic process forces 'selection' upon those who use it whether it be as playwright or as children improvising. Drama is not free as some advocates would have us believe. It is specific in its illustrations and brings the significant detail to the surface. This process of selection seems to me to be an essential one in the craft of writing as well and therefore the drama is able to help the English in the broad sense that it provides the microcosm which may then become the paragraph or the chapter and incidentally provides also the raw materials for skills work. For example, any of the passages transcribed here serve as a model from which the punctuation of direct speech may be taught. There are other areas, not so easily definable, in which this kind of improvised drama benefits the children who use it. It encourages oral fluency and demands considerable self-discipline and awareness of other individuals within a group. The amount of discussion required was particularly valuable as a means of encouraging listening ability and consideration of other views.

Written Work

While the dramatic improvisations continued for a period of weeks, each child spent some time writing a personal version of the story, a 'book' in chapters. This writing was certainly shaped and influenced by the drama although many of the incidents which found their way into these books never occurred in drama.

I was particularly keen to encourage these pupils to write something of greater length than they would normally produce, giving special attention to the skills of punctuation and paragraphing. I include here some examples from the 'books' of five of these pupils, A and B being above average for the group, C and D average, and E below average. Their work is fairly representative of the kind of work produced, but I do not wish to make any special claims about its quality or any effect the drama might have had on that aspect. What I do maintain, quite strongly, is that because of the 'here and now' quality of the drama, the writing was constantly fed and shaped in a more immediate and enjoyable way than would otherwise be possible, and that a complete book was written by each of the children, many of whom would produce only a few lines with little or no enthusiasm under the ordinary circumstances of an 'English' classroom. This is where the drama helped, through its direct involvement of the feeling.

Pupil A

The bell had gone and it is time to go home. Paul got in deep thought on the bus that evening thinking what to say to his parents. After tea that evening when all the things were cleared away he sat in the armchair and his mother

and father were on the sofa reading. He then said in a rather awkward way:
"Dad, I am old enough to leave home aren't I"
His dad peered over the paper.
"What makes you say that son."
"Well um."
"Come on out with it."
"Well I want to leave home."
"but . . ."
"Listen dad I thought I am old enough now to leave home but first I want my share of the family fortune."
"Now you listen to me, I agree you are old enough to leave home but what is this about family fortunes?"
"Well money really thats what I meant."
"Oh I see well here is the money."
And he pulled out a box from under the sofa he gave Paul a million or so pounds and then he said:
"I thought it might be coming to this and your mum is a bit upset but, well I suppose you are at a difficult age."
"I plan to leave this weekend okay."
"Yes son thats alright."
and no more was said about it that evening.

Pupil B – Paul's Money

It was a few days after Paul had arrived in London. He was sitting down in a Pub up Park Street having a small snack. He was in the corner reading a newspaper when two girls came and sat by him. Paul put down the newspaper and said,
"Hullo want to drink?"
"Yes please" said one of the girls "I'll have a gin and tonic please"
"I'll have one too" said the other girl.
So Paul went up to the bar and got the drinks and went back and sat at the table. Paul said:
"What's your names?"
One of the girls said
"I'm Jane and this is Ruth."
Paul said "Mine's Paul"
Then Jane said,
"We want to open up a hairdressing salon. We got the property and shop but now all the trouble is the inside because it really is in a bad state, and we want £200 to get the inside straighter out. And when we saw you we thought that you looked a nice young man who would help us"
Paul said "How do you know I have this 200 pounds to help you?"
"We don't but if you could give us as much as you can we can try and raise the rest to make the 200 pound."

Paul said "Is this all you want?"
Ruth said "I think that we will want more for our clothes which we'll work in and for our staff I say we'll want about 800 pounds"
"Yes now I come to think of it we will want that much"
"Well as a matter of fact I have that much and I will help you, but I want to go into more detail, can I come and see the old salon tomorrow?" said Paul.
The two girls said "Yes sure meet you in here tomorrow at 2 o'clock."
"Right I'll be waiting"

Pupil C
. . . .He arrived at London at quarter past 4 he pulled up a taxi and told him to go to the Savoy hotel. When he got there he ordered a room and a drink he saw a girl in the corner on a table on her own he fancied her. So he went over and said "Do you want a drink?"
She said "Yes I don't mind if I do Ill have a bacardi and coke". So he went over and got her it.
"What's your name" said Alan.
"Mary Johnson Whats yours"
"Alan Rodford are you doing anything tonight"
"No"
"Ill meet you at half past 8"
"OK" She said yes because she fancied him as well. Alan went up to his room and freshened up until 8.30. Alan took her to the theater and after for a meal. After the meal when Alan was walking Mary back to there hotel Mary's ex boyfriend saw them kissing and he said
"What do you think your doing with my girl"
Alan replied "Shes mine not yours. She may have been yours but shes mine now not yours"
"Shut your mouth or Ill fill it"
"You just try it" said Alan. Then a fight broke out they hit each other they rolled over on the floor this carried on for about half an hour then Alan walked back to the hotel.
When Alan felt for his wallet he found it wasn't there he swore a few times then told Mary.
"How much was in it"
"There was £200. I'll look for him tomorrow. Goodnight. Alan went to bed feeling depressed about the money but happy he had a good friend.

Pupil D – Spending His Money
Paul got up in the morning and went to a cafe and there he had a cup of tea and some biskites and then a man came in and said
"Excuse me sir we are hear to talk about stock cars we wondered if you would like to join a club"
And he went on talking about these cars and how much they needed, wich as

a matter of fact was £4,000 and they ended up by raging
"Well sir how about it would you like to join?"
"Yes I would I will put £4,000 with the sum you need?"
"By the way sir the club is held on Mondays, Wednesdays and Saturdays when would you like to come."
"Well it is Tuesday today. Tomorrow perhaps, would that do?"
"Yes sir I will pick you up at 2pm."
"By the way" said Dave as he was walking out of the door.
"I will have the money ready by tomorrow"

Pupil E – Stephen Writes a Letter Home
That morning Stephen counted up his money, he has only 150 pounds left that afternoon he decided to write a letter home asking his parents if he could go home because he was lonely and never had much money left. Then his mother received the letter, she was very pleased but his Father had doubts about letting him come home.
Because Stephen's father said to Stephen before he left that he wouldent be able to come back.
Finally they made a decision to let him come home.

PART TWO

RESEARCHING DRAMA

Denis Vincent

Although we now move from specific cases and illustrations to a more general kind of discussion, the two following sections do make a direct address to teachers; at the same time the serious researcher can draw a valuable moral from them. In Britain educational drama is largely unresearched but it is doubtful, as Jim Hoetker will show, that the conventional methods of educational research would have cast much light on many aspects of the subject in any case, had the resources ever been available in the first place. Thus if we wish to understand more about drama we can expect findings based on observational schedules, attitude and adjustment scales, interest inventories and personality and attainment tests to add only marginally to our understanding. Nor is it likely that these will provide any conclusive 'justification' for drama. The preceding sections have provided some informal examples of alternative ways in which one might set about understanding and evaluating drama. In doing so they have anticipated to some extent principles which the following authors try to make more explicit.

The teacher who has no interest in formally researching the subject will still benefit from the models for thinking about drama which Hoetker and Brossell provide. Pat Smyth has already hinted at the doubts which beset the teacher embarking on a drama lesson – 'I like doing drama, we can have a good muck about.' There is sometimes a pressing need for tools of analysis and interpretation. Even where a teacher does not find himself cast in the role of staff-room apologist for drama, sustained effective teaching requires constantly renewed insights into the on-going activities – 'formative' evaluation – in his drama teaching.

What follows can be read as essays about teaching drama and how individual teachers can set about interpreting their efforts. They are included however as a guide and encouragement to those wishing to undertake a more deliberate empirical study of educational drama, but who are dismayed or baffled by the seemingly inappropriate advice contained in the conventional introductory texts on research design. The school of humanistic or 'third force' psychology described by Gordon Brossell may be unfamiliar to teachers, but it is probably a more fruitful way of thinking about drama than those provided by experimental, behaviouristic and psychoanalytic psychology – or their popular caricatures – which teachers may recall from college courses.

One hopes also that if the concerns raised by preceding contributions have succeeded in attracting the attention of the full-time educational researcher, the following sections will indicate how research might be conducted in a way meaningful to the practising teacher.

CHAPTER 5.

RESEARCHING DRAMA: AN AMERICAN VIEW

James Hoetker

1. Prefatory. What follows is an attempt to say something about the sorts of research into educational drama that might pay off, and about the sorts that are a waste of time.

To start autobiographically: I was lucky enough to finish my graduate work at a time when there was briefly in Washington an administration that was expressing its belief in both education and the arts through the provision of unprecedentedly large amounts of money to support development of arts-in-education programmes. I fell into one of these programmes, an endeavour called the Educational Laboratory Theatre Project (ELTP), which had upwards of $6 million to spend between 1966 and 1970 to subsidize three professional repertory companies and to provide for periodic attendance at the theatres by several hundred thousand secondary school students.

The ELTP was conceived of as an experiment and even, wistfully, as a pilot project. So a research and evaluation component was built into it, to be managed by federally-supported educational laboratory.

I ended up directing this research and evaluation of the ELTP, with an annual budget that at times exceeded a quarter-million dollars. With that sort of money, one can assemble a large and expert staff and can hire the very best advice. Which we did. At the end of the ELTP, the laboratory issued a Final Report that ran over a thousand pages in four volumes and was supplemented by two special reports and several volumes of curriculum materials.

During the run of the ELTP, we did everything we knew how to do by way of research. We gathered and analysed great piles of documents of all sorts; we administered and readministered questionnaires to thousands of people and interviewed hundreds more; we solicited written and oral opinions from educators, public figures, parents, students, actors; we hired theatre people and drama educators and sent them around to observe and write reports for us; we analysed curriculum materials, held symposia and workshops, and even sponsored an essay contest.

We tape recorded audience responses during plays and student talk on the buses home from the theatre; we used semantic differentials to compare the 'meanings' of the theatre experience to boys and girls, blacks and whites, teachers and students, actors and audiences; we devised and adapted various projective tests and content-analysed student responses to them; we developed and used tests of achievement in drama; we conducted the largest and most expensive single experimental study of English teaching that has, so far as I know, ever been carried out. And so on.

At the conclusion of all this activity – which was, I must admit, exciting and a great deal of fun – when the time came to write prefaces and conclusions to all our assembled volumes of evidence, I found that I had become, along with others on the staff, a pronounced sceptic about the value of the 'scientific' research that we had done. Indeed, the most useful parts of our reports, for one interested in understanding the programme and its successes and failures, were the comments of the students and the informed insights of the expert observers.

The 'Studies' volume of the ELTP Final Report, reflecting the state of mind into which we had fallen and our resolution to be as honest as possible about what we had and had not done, began like this:

> 'There is an unwritten rule of the research trade that one must give his reader the impression that the study being reported moved smoothly, step by step, from hypothesis formation through design and execution and data analysis to interpretation. A *persona* must be created who speaks in the third person omniscient and is never surprised by anything that happens, because everything goes just as it was planned .... This prologue is for two reasons. First of all, it is an occasion for apologizing in advance for falling occasionally into the pose of omniscient objectivity, and to assure the reader that when we do so we are lying. Second, it is an occasion for noting that this volume contains only a fraction of the .... research done on the ... Project – that part which we [thought good for our careers to get in print]. Other studies that were carried out have never been written up – either because they were seriously deficient or because our data collection plans were irremediably scrambled up by accidents of various sorts . . .'

The general introduction to the Report further contained the following paragraphs, which are worth quoting, though fumblingly expressed, in that these propositions are, I believe, much to the present point:

> 'Some of those involved in planning and managing the Project spoke of the theatre experience as one that could humanize both people and institutions; or they talked about the vapidity of a life without art . . .; or they talked of richness of experience and

empathy and insight and appreciation and creativity; or they talked about the sociological imperative to find constructive options to self-destructive uses of our ever-increasing amounts of leisure time. These people hoped that CEMREL (the laboratory) would find ways to demonstrate that changes in these areas indeed came about as a result of the . . . Project.

We have not, of course, been able to do any such thing. With the rest of the human race, lettered and unlettered, we share the inability to operationalize or objectify such elusive and internal phenomena. The studies in this report will inevitably be disappointing to those who hoped . . . that a well-endowed research component could, in three years or so, get us further along than Aristotle and Hume and Cant and Groce have been able to do. . . ..

Nontrivial changes in perceptions, tastes, and life styles that may be attributable to artistic experiences are qualitatively different from easily measurable (and often trivial) changes in knowledge, attitudes, and skills. We know of some few students who were dramatically changed by the ELT Project experiences . . .. But for most people the effects of an artistic experience, or a series of them, remain, as it were, a form of potential energy only, and have their effects far in the future, as traces of them are impinged upon by and interact with other life experiences. The residue of an artistic experience may have no observable effect upon a person's life until there have been enough other experiences for a sort of critical mass to be reached. Alternatively the artistic experience, may itself be a catalytic agent, making sense out of series of other sorts of experiences. In any case, it will be the extremely rare occasion when it is possible to attribute a change in a person to particular set of aesthetic experiences.'

Our discontents were leading us to question, and eventually to reject entire, the natural science model of experimental research that we had commonly in our graduate schools been given to understand was THE ONLY WAY TO TRUTH. At the time, though, we still felt guilty about our doubting – feeling, as we had been taught to feel, that all our graphs of student reactions, our observational reports, our subjective analyses of the human and institutional complexities of the programme were somehow inferior to and less respectable than those studies that tested hypotheses and issued in statistical arrays and significance tests – even when the latter studies turned up nothing of interest. Today, I would argue that almost the opposite is the case.

2. The Political Uses of Research. Educators tend to believe – are in fact trained to believe – that the accumulation of research evidence can serve the cause of education by convincing policy-makers to support programmes which are demonstrably superior. Research evidence is thought to be increasingly effective for such ends, to the extent that it is quantitative, gathered according to rigorous designs, and presented in form of great arrays of statistics.

I submit that things seldom work that way. Rather, as Shipman puts it, in *The Limitations of Social Research* (1972):

> 'Once a report is available policy makers tend to use it selectively. Results are used when they support the views of politicians and ignored when they do not . . .. Where the evidence fails to support policies already agreed on it is ignored or described as inexplicable or opposed to common knowledge. The sequence is not consideration of evidence and then decision, but decision and then the mustering of evidence.' (p. 155)

A much more effective strategy for justifying a programme of gaining support involves devising ways of giving policy-makers actual or vicarious experiences of the programme. The most effective single programme evaluation that I know of was prepared for an Artist-in-Residence programme, and it was by way of a short, beautifully photographed and sensitively edited colour film of the artists working and interacting with students. Probably the kinescopes, widely circulated in the United States both by The National Council of Teachers of English (NCTE) and by commercial distributors, of the BBC series on Creative Drama has done more than any single other thing to arouse real interest in drama and to convince educators of its value.

The documentary film *High School* has probably contributed more than any ten research reports to the cause of school reform. More effective than all the statistics a computer can print in a week, so far as convincing people of the value of drama, would be to involve head teachers and administrators and legislators in expertly conducted drama sessions; or to let them watch children at drama and talk to the children afterwards; or if nothing else is possible, to show them tapes and films of good drama and let them read and see the products of drama sessions.

3. The Limitations of Experimental Research. There are two not unrelated grounds on which one may object to representations of hypothesis testing experiments as the only respectable mode of scientific research in education. First, there is the empirical ground that conventional experiments have not produced enough useful information to justify the time and money that has gone into them. Then, there is the theoretical ground that the assumptions under-lying the experimental model are inadequate to the reality.[1]

M.D. Shipman, in the valuable little book already cited, demonstrated the inability of conventional research methods to produce consistent answers even to the most direct sorts of educational questions. Reviewing the contradictory results of British research on i.t.a. *v.* traditional orthography and on streamed *v.* unstreamed classes, Shipman remarks that, given the straight-forward nature of the questions, 'the inconclusive outcome of all this effort is a warning of the limitations of existing research methods in providing answers that can be trusted as a basis for policy' (p. 91). Shipman then goes on to note two other curious things about the process of 'objective' research in the real world of subjective researchers. First, that the results of a particular study may often be predicted on the basis of the proclivities of the sponsoring organization or the ideology of the investigator. (Another writer, some years ago, noted the curious circumstance that short published studies of progressive *v.* traditional educational practices favoured progressive methods, while larger-scale studies tended to favour traditional methods or to find no differences. He concluded that short studies that did not buttress the presuppositions of the investigators about the superiority of progressive practices were never offered for publication, but that so much time and money had been devoted to the larger studies that they had to be published no matter what their conclusions.)

Second, Shipman notes that the failure of research to settle anything does not in the least 'disturb the confidence in research to come up with conclusive comparisons.' The critics 'do not conclude that the available techniques were too blunt to measure differences' but instead press confidently for more research. We are here, in other words, involved not with science, but with articles of faith in science, and of science very narrowly conceived. To wit: that the manifest failure of behavioural research to produce answers to educational questions is a positive argument for the proposition that bigger and better behavioural research *must* produce those answers. To paraphrase a Father of the Church, 'Because it is absurd, we believe.'

Shipman's criticisms of social research apply primarily to the old-fashioned 'horserace' model of the research process. Is curriculum Man-of-War speedier than curriculum *Secretariat*? Is *drama* better than *recitation*? More sophisticated multivariate designs, however, which allow for simultaneous evaluations of the effects of many independent variables and interactions on

[1] The remarks made here about experimental studies apply as well to a great many descriptive and correlational studies of education matters. Specifically, to those that are more concerned with matters of form and procedure – sample size and selection, reliability of measurements, statistical analyses, generalizability of findings, and so on – than with matters of substance and consequence validity of measurements, practical importance, the 'fit' between the questions being asked and the methods being employed by the investigator, and so on.

many dependent variables, so far do not have any better a record of providing dependable answers.

To take two examples. A study of my own sought to discover the effects upon students' responses to plays of different methods of preparing students for the plays (published by NCTE as *Students as Audiences*). It involved 50 teachers and 3,000 students. It was designed by one of the top research statisticians in the country, with the design allowing for the evaluation of several thousand hypotheses about relationships between 16 variations in teaching procedures and some dozen measures of student response. The study cost more than $30,000, not counting the salaries of the regular project staff. Almost all of the familiar 'alternative explanations' for any results we might discover had been anticipated and controlled for.

Despite all this fuss and trouble, and despite some commonsensical positive findings – such as that students who studied plays most intensively enjoyed them less and recalled less about them – the limping conclusion of the whole effort was this:

> 'the results of the present experiment do not support the positions taken either by educators or theatre people about the effects of different classroom practices as clearly as either group might have wished. Each group, however, may take comfort from particular findings and each may care to take thought about what seems to be the relative impotence of classroom instruction to either inhibit or facilitate short-range student behaviours of the sorts measured in this study.'

The report of an even more ambitious, impeccably designed study, ten years in the doing and directed by Alan Purves for the International Educational Assessment, was recently published under the title *Literature Education in Ten Countries (1973)*. The effects upon literary achievement and preference of some 600-odd personal, educational, and social variables were evaluated in this remarkable study. By far the greater part of the variations in all the contrasts was explained by a small cluster of variables related to home background – students wise enough to be born into advantaged homes were better literature students than those who had not been so discriminating in their choices of parents. So Purves (as I had earlier) found himself scrabbling desperately to avoid the conclusion that nothing schools and teachers do makes much difference in pupil achievement in literature.

Theoretical objections to quantitative, controlled, hypothesis-testing research are based on the simple proposition that human beings and human social organisms are different in kind from rocks, gases, rats, and pigeons and cannot be comprehended by models that conceive of them as nothing but more complicated rocks, gases, rats, and pigeons. It does not necessarily follow from a rejection of oversimplified models of man (as some humanists would like to have it, and be done with the whole bother) that the scientific study of man and his creations should be abandoned. Rather it means that the homage done to reliability and control needs to be suspended for a duration during which a great deal of inspired empirical mucking around takes place, and that methods need to be cobbled that are adequate to describing and reporting human phenomena in all their holistic complexity.

The commitment to repeatability, generalizability, quantification, and control leads, in practice, to research studies that investigate not what is important, but what is economically measurable according to our poor and stunted psychometric technology.[1] Things of real interest to educators – appreciation, understanding, humaneness, self-respect, creativity, sensitivity – are largely uninvestigated simply because these things cannot be operationalized in terms of external behaviours observable at the experimenter's convenience. Or if studied, such things are operationalized in terms of scores on available instruments of dubious relevance to the phenomenon in its naturalistic, real world manifestations.

There is little to be gained in persisting in these ways. And there is really no necessity for either such persistence or for the abandonment of the ideal of scientifically investigating what happens in, for instance, drama.

4. Some Alternative Modes of Research. My foregoing objections against the use of natural science models of research in investigations of human beings are (as many readers certainly have recognized) several decades out of date, insofar as the natural sciences themselves generally have abandoned the idea that wholes can be understood through the process of controlled study of their parts in isolation. The key terms today in the sciences today are 'systems' and 'holistic.'

Ervin Laszlo puts the situation this way, in *The Systems View of the World* (1972):

> 'In the history of Western science, atomistic and holistic ways of thinking have alternated . . . We witness today another shift in ways of thinking: the shift toward rigorous but holistic theories. This means thinking in terms of facts and events in the context of

[1] It has been my experience – which each reader may check against his own – that it is the investigators and doctoral advisers in the 'softer' educational disciplines who are most likely to be hung up on form and to be narrow and dogmatic about 'proper' ways to conduct educational research, while those who are really at home with the theoretical and mathematical bases of research design, and therefore beyond being intimidated by the prospect of violating dimly apprehended 'laws' of research, are much likelier to be seriously concerned with matters of real-world meaning and practical import. 'A little knowledge' and all that. B.F. Skinner, I have been told, discourages his doctoral students from talking statistics. This might be one behaviouristic example it would be good for humanistic educators to follow – since it seems unlikely we can make all professors and their doctoral students into proficient mathematical statisticians.

wholes, forming integrated sets with their own properties and relationships. Looking at the world in terms of such sets of integrated relations constitutes the systems view. It is the present and next choice over atomism, mechanism, and specialization. (p.19)

'Contemporary science tends increasingly to concentrate on organization: not what a thing is *per se*, nor how one thing produces an effect on one other thing, but rather how sets of events are structured and how they function in relation to their 'environment' – other sets of things, likewise structured in space and time.' (p.20)

Many of the leaders in educational research and evaluation have recently been coming around to the same holistic point of view. But the objections had to be stated, I believe, because of the cultural lag that, for many reasons, afflicts experimental psychology and positivistic sociology and, consequently, educational research, which borrows so many of its tools and models and doctrines from these disciplines.

In the space remaining, I would like to call the reader's attention to just three approaches to educational research that are based on holistic, rather than behaviouristic, models of mankind and of knowledge. These approaches – and other similar ones that have been developing in other disciplines – are, I submit, much more likely to produce useful knowledge about such topics as drama than are old-style educational experiments.

Humanistic psychologists, first, are interested primarily in normal healthy persons, rather than in the ill or abnormal, and so they face in their work methodological problems remarkably similar to those faced by one trying to research drama. Following Maslow, these psychologists have found it more accurate to use the term 'discovery' in place of the term 'research' to describe their approach to obtaining scientific knowledge. Gordon Brossell deals with their 'heuristic research strategies' in a following essay.

Approaching the problem of understanding aesthetic responses from another psychological tradition – that of Freudian psychoanalysis – Norman H. Holland (1973), outlines a method and a theoretical structure for studying responses to literature that should be helpfully suggestive to researchers who are, like several of the authors represented in this volume, already engaged in the naturalistic analysis of tape recordings of children engaged in drama.

Holland's study, which represents both an extension of his ideas in *The Dynamics of Literary Response* (1968) and a renunciation of his former allegiance to the ideals of objectivity and repeatability, has as its raw materials H.D's retrospective account of her analysis with Freud (*Tribute to Freud*, 1956) and some five hundred pages of transcribed conversations about literature with each of a small number of his students.

Holland's research has led him to a theory of the literary transaction which involves four propositions. First, just as one lives by creating variations of an identity theme, so one takes in experience through it, and this leads to the principle that each reader tries to compose from the elements of the work a match to his own characteristic style. Second, the reader admits elements of the work into his mental functioning only to the extent that he can shape them 'into his characteristic pattern of defence or adaptation.' Third, 'once he has admitted them, he uses the elements he has taken in to create a fantasy of the type that matters to him.' And finally, by means of the defences he has matched, he transforms that fantasy toward a moral, esthetic or intellectual 'point' that enables him to find in the work unity, significance, and pleasure (p.145).

As to the methods of the research which gave rise to these theoretical propositions, Holland has this to say:

> 'One is driven to the analysis of personality and response in depth, with all the loss of experimental isolation that entails. Ordinary experiments become pointless because there is no ordinary pattern of causation to test out. We are confronted instead with the complex, overdetermined systems of our own style or reacting with the world.
>
> What we do have – and it is a far richer source of data, I think, than any numbers, even the most multivariate of matrices – is the actual words of the poem and the actual words [my students and I] used about the poem, together with their introspections and your and my experience of all of this. We are, in effect, in the position of psychoanalysts interpreting a patient's free associations to a dream . . . .
>
> The analyst lets his patient talk freely, and he listens for recurring themes in what he hears, mingling his own subjective experience of the patient with what the patient objectively says out loud. Finally, he arrives at an interpretation by understanding those themes as converging toward a single, central issue.' (pp. 156–157)

Holland's book, and the fuller and more technical presentation of his work that is forthcoming under the title *Five Readers Reading*, can serve the researcher in drama both as a model of a difficult task well done and as a rich source of ideas. As an alternative to the atomistic natural science models of research, it offers a holistic model based on psychoanalytic practice. Quoting W.W. Meissner, Holland formulates the principles underlying this practice in terms that should be especially congenial to educators in literature and drama.

'Analysis is not concerned with the repeatability of data from case to case, but rather with the inner consistency and pattern of meaning that obtains within each case. Meaning is the central fact of human experience . . . . . . The whole direction of the therapist's effort is toward elaboration of the full context of meaning in which the whole range of data that he has gathered about the patient falls into a consistent, coherent, and intelligible pattern.' (pp.157)

The research techniques of both the humanistic psychologist and the psychoanalyst proceed primarily by way of intensive case studies of a few individuals. But the researcher – especially when engaged in the practical business of evaluating programmes – must often deal with groups and not individuals.

An analogue to the psychologists' holistic studies of individuals can be found in the methodologies developed by field anthropologists for studying cultural groups. In an address on 'Anthropological Research Models' to an NCTE Seminar on Research Design, Carol Talbert (1973) discussed anthropological investigations of educational institutions:

'The ideal way to do anthropology in schools would be to become a student, sit all day, take orders from the teacher, visit other students in their homes, and play with them. The ideal way to study the culture of teachers would be to be a teacher oneself. Yet, as researchers, we cannot be children or well-socialized teachers . . . . The alternative is to be a tolerated onlooker, participating as much as allowable in everyday customary activities. We can ask many questions, follow people around, become part of the scenery and hopefully be taken for granted. We can hope people cease structuring their interactions to fit our expectancies . . .. Field work gives the meaning, from the children's point of view, of the children's actions. These meanings are not on a conscious level and to expect to glean them from interviews and questionnaires is simplistic.' (pp.191–2)

The three major contributions of field anthropology, according to Talbert, are participant-observer methodology, a comparative, cross-cultural perspective, and a relativistic view of culture and cultural patterns. One taking an anthropological approach to the study of educational drama would, in effect, be setting out to learn what drama means to the students and their teachers. What do they see themselves doing during and as a result of drama? 'The essence of the anthropologist's task is to discover the categories which informants use. What are their categories and what do they mean? How is their knowledge organized and classified? Answering these questions is what discovering culture is all about.' (Talbert, p.98).

The process of discovering what drama means in the lives of the students, the teachers, and their school will involve the investigator in interacting with the students and teachers and being accepted by them.[1] It will involve locating several informants who will explain, answer questions, and correct the investigator's tentative formulations. It will involve the recording, for later comparison and analysis, as much as possible of everything that is seen and said and thought. Beyond this, according to the investigator's ingenuity and purposes, any number of activities and techniques may be used for gathering data. Documents may be examined; videotapes may be made and analysed for patterns of interaction or judged for quality by expert informants; discussions and dramatic dialogues and informal talk may be tape-recorded and analysed to determine whether there are linguistic conventions peculiar to drama; systems of coding dramatic activities may be devised, so that variations in lessons and sequences can be better described and related to participants' experiences. Audio or videotapes of drama sessions can be viewed with students or groups of students, with the resulting conversations recorded as still additional data. Any existing research tool, actually, can be used that will not damage the rapport between the investigator and his subjects.

The report of such a study would attempt to give the reader a version of the investigator's own experience, of the process by which he learned, as well as what he learned, and it would undoubtedly be augmented by lengthy quotations from the evidence on which the investigator's formulations are based.

Such a report would resemble a journalistic account, an autobiography, or even a novel more than a conventional research report. It would differ from these, perhaps, primarily in that the author's subjectivity would be decreased and controlled by his methodology and his discipline's rules of evidence.

Louis M. Smith pioneered this sort of educational research – what he calls the 'microethnography of the classroom' – in the study reported in *The Complexities of an Urban Classroom* (1968). In Smith's particular approach, the movement is toward the formulation of visual models of the activities, rituals and interactions observed, which models are then compared and

[1] Connie and Harold Rosen's *The Language of Primary School Children* (Penguin Education, 1973) is a beautiful example of what can be done along this line by investigators sensitive and serious and painstaking enough. The Rosens' approach is commonsensical and eclectic. In their hands it works. I would, however, differ with the Rosen's unnecessarily humble disclaimer that 'their project plan did not call for anything which would be dignified by the name of research'. It is, on the contrary, research of a very high order, and the disclaimer is an unpleasing documentation of the usurpation of the honorific term 'research' by one narrow sect. The Rosens' Chapter 5, 'In Search of Drama: More Questions than Answers', is a good example of just the sort of 'descriptive and critical' research into drama that Brossell and I are trying to promote in the present essays.

synthesized and related in various ways, so that larger and larger segments of the classroom social system may be comprehended in a single coherent model. Smith's book, and his more recent writings on 'microethnography' as a method for evaluation, should like Holland's work, be a valuable source of ideas for one engaged in researching drama.

5. Evaluating Drama Programmes. 'Researching drama' is a special case of 'researching human behaviour' which is a big can of worms. Which is why this paper has taken so long in getting to that special case of 'researching drama' that is probably of most interest to the reader, namely, evaluating drama programmes.

So let me deal with that little can of worms by way of conclusion. I hope we agree by now that there is little place in the evaluation of a drama programme for the sort of evaluation that begins with behavioural objectives treated as experimental hypotheses (i.e., Treatment A will cause behaviours J, N, O, and P to occur in X amounts at time Y). Depending on the sort of drama we are interested in evaluating, though, and on what it is we are trying to learn for whom, there are a range of evaluation strategies from which we may choose.

A distinction may first be made according to the audience for the evaluation report. A 'formative evaluation' (to use Michael Scriven's term) is addressed to the actual participants in a programme, and it provides information for the purpose of helping to improve the ongoing programme. (A formative evaluation would not even necessarily make use of an independent evaluator, though one would be desirable on the grounds that a teacher cannot do two things at once, that two heads are better than one, and so forth). Since formative evaluation information must be conveyed quickly and continuously if it is to be used, reports of formative evaluations are likely to be informal, even though the evaluator's methods need not be.

A 'summative evaluation' does require an independent evaluator. It is addressed to audiences besides those actually involved in a programme, but interested in or affected by it – administrators, education officers, funding agencies, parents. The report of a summative evaluation, taking account of the informational needs and the values of the audiences, will be more formal, must contain descriptive information, and may contain judgments and recommendations.

Though this is oversimplified, it may be helpful to think of a formative evaluation as addressed to an audience concerned primarily with 'what is happening'; of a summative evaluation as addressed to those who want to know 'what happened'; and of a research report as addressed to people who are most interested in 'what will happen if . . .'. But these distinctions do not necessarily imply anything about either methodology or form of reporting.

The form of reporting depends in part on the methodology of the evaluation and in part on the needs and nature of the audience. A perfectly respectable research or evaluation report, I am urging, might in particular cases take the form, for example, of demonstrations by students or displays of student work; films; multimedia shows; transcriptions of tape-recorded conversations; fictions based on the evaluator's experiences; videotape recordings; or a series of simulations designed to give the audience a vicarious experience of the programme in question. Robert Stake's article on 'responsive evaluations' of arts programmes in the Fall, 1973 *Journal of Aesthetic Education* is an excellent discussion of these possibilities, by a recent convert from hardnosed statistical evaluation.

As to methodology in evaluation, it will depend to a large extent on the sort of drama we are evaluating. Let us say that any particular instance of drama may be located, at least in comparison to other instances of drama, on a grid, one of the co-ordinates of which runs from 'instrumental' (i.e. for the sake of some other educational end) to 'intrinsic' (i.e. for its own sake), and the other of which runs from 'completely spontaneous' to 'completely planned out.' It should be clear that an instance of drama that would be located well toward the 'instrumental' and 'planned out' ends of the co-ordinates would be much more amenable to what we have called conventional scientific evaluation than an instance located off towards the 'intrinsic' and 'spontaneous' ends of the co-ordinates – the latter case calling for the intuitive, involved, qualitative, meaning-seeking discovery strategies we have discussed.

Even in the case of a use of drama such as that made in Ray Verrier's ingenious lessons on Chief David that are discussed earlier in this volume, where drama is being used instrumentally and the teacher has a clear idea at the start of what he wants to happen, the evaluator still has a choice of two general strategies.

On the one hand, the investigator could ascertain the teacher's objectives and then devise ways to gather data to establish the extent to which the objectives were attained. Verrier's objectives could be stated in terms of descriptions of a series of experiences – cognitive, linguistic, manipulatory, and so on – that the teacher deems it educationally desirable for the students to have at the particular time. The evaluator's major contribution, in such a situation, might be to identify those students who were or were not indeed having the desired experiences and perhaps further to provide observations about the problems or positive and negative contributions of particular students during the experiences – information it is not always possible for the teacher himself to gather at the right time or in sufficient detail.

On the other hand, the evaluator might be given no information at all about the objectives or the intentions of the teacher, but would simply be invited in to observe and participate. The evaluator's report would then consist of an account of what he thought he had seen happening and his inferences about who was learning what. The crucial issue in such a 'goal-free evaluation' (again, Michael Scriven's term) would be the extent to which the evaluator's observations matched the teacher's intentions – the extent to which the drama had the same meaning to both. (The evaluation, that is to say, would involve 'doing anthropology' with the teacher as one of the evaluator's informants and the evaluator as one of the teacher's.)

Probably the best source of ideas on programme evaluation – though the book is a mixed bag – is the encyclopaedic *Handbook on Formative and Summative Evaluation of Student Learning* (1971), edited by Bloom, Hastings, and Madaus. The chapters by Kamii, Cazden, Foley, Moore and Kennedy, and Purves, especially, deal with issues of concern to drama specialists.

7. Coda. The burden of this paper has not been that reason and 'science' should be rejected as a means to knowledge about drama, but simply 1) that we know too little to afford the luxury of objectivity and 2) that we will get nowhere if we restrict ourselves to techniques of research that are suited only to the ratrunner's model of the human being, which everyone knows by direct personal experience is comically inadequate, but which many of us have been trained to accept as a convention because it is 'useful'. I no longer think that it is.

REFERENCES

BLOOM, B.S., HASTINGS, J.T., and MADAUS, G.F. (1971). *Handbook on Formative and Summative Evaluation of Student Learning*. New York: McGraw-Hill.

'H.D.' (1956). *Tribute to Freud*. New York: Pantheon Books.

HOLLAND, N.H. (1968). *The Dynamics of Literary Response*. London: Oxford University Press.

HOLLAND, N.H. (1973). *Poems in Person*. New York: W.W. Norton.

HOLLAND, N.H. (in press). *Five Readers Reading*. New Haven: Yale.

LASZLO, E. (1972). *The Systems View of the World*. New York: Brazziller.

PURVES, A. (1973). *Literature Education in Ten Countries. International Studies in Education II*. New York, London: Wiley.

SHIPMAN, M.D. (1972). *The Limitations of Social Research*. London: Longmans.

SMITH, L.M. (1968). *The Complexities of an Urban Classroom*. New York: Holt, Rinehart and Winston.

TALBERT, C. (1973). 'Anthropological Research Models', *Research in the Teaching of English*, Fall, 1973.

CHAPTER 6

RESEARCHING DRAMA: A HUMANISTIC PERSPECTIVE

Gordon C. Brossell

I feel, along with many others, that we can and need to arrive at a much firmer understanding of the use and effect of drama in the classroom. And I agree with Hoetker that no one is going to learn anything very important about drama in education if, to be respectable, he must use the sanctioned tools of orthodox research. I had rather talk about 'discovering' than 'researching.' Someone interested in making discoveries about things operates very differently from the experimenter. He has little in the way of established method to follow and so must rely on some peculiarly human qualities – intuition, insight, imagination, curiosity, speculation, hope – rather than on a set of acquired skills. He must become open to and engaged with the phenomenal world of his investigations, since his own unique view of things is the empirical basis for the discoveries he makes. His major resource, in short, is himself.

A chief objection to the discoverer, of course, is that he is not scientific (while the researcher is). Yet both contribute to our knowledge, and the invidious distinction between them is more a matter of cultural bias than anything else. The knowledge each generates *is* different, however, and we should understand the nature and significance of each kind before we decide how best to explore drama.

Knowledge generated by the application of classical research methods tends, first of all, to be *abstract* since it is not felt firsthand but witnessed by a spectator. It is therefore *descriptive*, since the observer must report what he sees. Research knowledge is also *atomistic* because of the scientist's concentration on specific elements of the object of examination. Thus it tends towards *generalizations* that are organized in logical, rational structures, categories, and taxonomies.

The knowledge of discovery is another matter. It is essentially *experiential*, since it arises out of direct contact and involvement with the phenomenal field of investigation. It is *random* and *subjective* as well, given the relative absence of predictability and control, and the necessity for personal judgment insures that it is *evaluative*. Such knowledge can also be called *holistic*, because it reflects a viewpoint that stresses organic unity.

My point about the two kinds of knowledge is this: They are different but not mutually exclusive. Experiential knowledge is the basis upon which the conceptual knowledge of science is built. No scientist can really pursue knowledge in an entirely objective way, without recourse to many of the distinctively human qualities – intuition, speculation, a 'sixth sense,' etc. – that characterize all our attempts to comprehend reality. In the words of Abraham Maslow (1970) in *The Psychology of Science*, experiential knowledge is necessary but not sufficient: It makes possible the development of abstract knowledge, which is necessary for life itself and for the fullest and richest development of human nature. Putting it another way experiential – or concrete – knowledge is prior to scientific – or abstract – knowledge but does not, in its unrefined state, allow us to broaden and deepen our understanding. We need both the raw, unshaped material of experience and the organizational power of abstraction for the fullest kinds of knowledge.

The recent work of several American psychologists makes much the same point. Maslow argues for the humanization of science through a synthesis of the knowledge gained through classical methodology and that gleaned by human empathy and understanding. Robert Ornstein (1973), in *The Psychology of Consciousness*, similarly identifies two major modes of human consciousness – one of them analytic, rational, verbal, and 'day-like'; the other holistic, intuitive, mystic, and 'night-like' – and says there must be a complementary interaction of the two if man is to realize his highest potential. Andrew Weil's *The Natural Mind* (1972) makes a similar statement. All of these writers are indebted, of course, to the seminal work in the field, Michael Polanyi's *Personal Knowledge* (1958).

An ideal investigative technique would use the concrete experiential data of personal discovery as a basis for later systematic analysis and classification. Our first priority should then be to develop not more sensitive, sophisticated instruments of measurement, but more sensitive, sophisticated knowers.

How shall we conduct our investigations into the use and effect of drama, then? I believe that among the best paradigms for researching drama are those that come from the so-called third force, or humanistic, psychologies (which are themselves a reaction against the scientific orthodoxy of behaviourism and Freudian psychoanalysis).

Drama is essentially a creative activity grounded in the personal experiences and individual personalities of its participants, in a context of social interaction. It is concerned, to borrow Brian Way's (1971) apt expression, with the 'uniqueness of each human essence.' The effect of drama is felt in an integral way, is on the whole person, as it were, and the learning it promotes is likely to be learning about oneself and one's relation to others. This is not to ignore the more conventional kinds of learning it may stimulate – understanding literature and improving language usage, for example – but to distinguish between its primary and secondary effects. It is the nature of dramatic activities to help people come to grips with their own feelings, outlooks, dispositions, abilities, and limitations – to get in closer touch with their real selves, to come to know themselves better. The study of drama, then, cannot be separated from the study of people.

Drama is both experience – what is actually happening – and a concept – of abstraction of experience. In the latter sense it is like other abstractions of experience we all know and label and talk about but must apprehend in our own unique, individual ways: love, honesty, prejudice, truth, disappointment, satisfaction, growth, and so on. Conceptual knowledge of drama can only come from experiential knowledge of drama. And experiential knowledge can be verified only by experiencing. If we discredit the subjective knowledge of personal involvement because it cannot be substantiated by conventional scientific means, we deny the very effects we are trying to study and understand.

Humanistic research begins with the subjective knowledge of experience, and discovery is its characteristic mode of inquiry. While it has no standard methodology, its advocates share a common attitude concerning the nature of the investigative task. This attitude has three recognizable aspects: 1) a problem-centered orientation, 2) the use of 'heuristic' methods of exploration, and 3) the holistic analysis of experiential data.

The humanistic researcher begins with a problem – the recognition of some situation or issue about which he knows little or nothing and wants to know more because he considers it important or interesting or valuable to do so. He does not know whether his findings will be commensurate with his original interest, but he attends to his own values in selecting an issue for investigation. Usually the problem arises out of questions to which standard research can supply no answers. When Abraham Maslow's work in psychopathology led him to ask questions about healthy people, for example, he found himself face to face with the problem of normality: Is good psychological health normal, or is it just as normal to suffer to some degree from psychological ill health? And even more important, how is the condition of normality affected by our *conception* of it?

As the humanistic researcher becomes increasingly involved in the subject of his investigations, he begins to sense its nature and to discriminate among the various aspects of his phenomenal field. He operates, in short, in a way which allows him continuously to make discoveries about his subject and to penetrate more closely to its essential nature. Just exactly how he does this is a matter for personal judgment and selection. Research of this kind has been called 'heuristic' and can be better understood by looking at an example of its use.

In 1961 the American psychologist-teacher Clark Moustakas published a book entitled *Loneliness*, an account of his own extended research into that subject. Moustakas was moved to undertake the study as a result of an intensely personal experience with loneliness: having to decide the question of his daughter's undergoing heart surgery, which could restore her health or result in her death. In his study, Moustakas moved progressively from the introspective soul searching of private crisis to observation of and engagement in the loneliness of others to the study of literary accounts of personal loneliness. When he felt he had grasped the essence of this particular condition of human experience, he presented his discoveries in *Loneliness*.

Writing later about his work, Moustakas identified a number of stages through which his heuristic research moved. First, there was the crisis of the original problem; second, a searching of the self, from which emerged a recognition of the significance of loneliness and its exploration; third, an expanding awareness of the subject through increased openness to it; fourth, an immersion of the self in the subject so that it became the center of the explorer's world; fifth, an intuitive grasping of the patterns and associations of loneliness until an integrated vision of it emerged; sixth, additional clarification and refinement of this understanding through examination of other work on the subject; and seventh, the creation of a form by which to express the investigator's findings.

Maslow's pioneering work in self-actualization used similar heuristic methods of research. In studying the personalities of psychologically healthy people, Maslow developed a positive, growth-oriented theory of human motivation that has become the basis for an alternative view of human nature to that of behaviourism. Describing his study in *Motivation and Personality*, (1970), Maslow distinguishes holistic analysis from that used in orthodox psychological research:

> 'We can conceive either that we are studying a discrete entity, or that we are studying a part of a whole. The former method we may call reductive-analytic. The latter we may call holistic-analytic. One essential characteristic of holistic analysis of the personality in actual practice is that there be a preliminary study or understanding of the total organism, and that we then proceed to study the role that our part of the whole plays in the organization and dynamics of the total organism.' (p.297)

A chief technique of holistic analysis is the process of *iteration*, used by Maslow in his investigation of personality syndromes. Starting with a non-technical, 'folk definition' conception, the investigator collects and organizes various extant usages of it and begins to define the conception more precisely. In light of the corrected definition, a first group of subjects is studied and the resulting information is applied to formulate a new definition more accurate than the preceding one. The evidence taken from succeeding groups goes to refine the original conception even further in a continuous process of self-correction.

If we are going to do research in drama – that is, if we are going systematically to gather information about its uses and effects, analyse that information, and draw conclusions from it – one good way to proceed would be to adopt the basic orientation of the humanistic researcher.

What would the humanistic researcher actually do, though, in exploring drama? Ultimately, specific operations would need to be worked out in each instance of research, since the conditions, the interests, and the people will vary. Let me just attempt to describe one way a humanistic researcher might tackle the subject, offering the example more in the hope of pointing directions than of prescribing techniques.

Humanistic psychologists have devoted considerable time and effort to studying the phenomenon of psychic energy and its expression in altered or heightened states of experience. Maslow's concept of the 'peak experience,' for example, describes the best moments in life, moments of ecstasy, rapture, and bliss – the moments of greatest happiness. A similar yet more inclusive construct is that called the 'Minerva experience,' developed by Herbert A. Otto (1967). Otto describes this concept as 'a network of highly formative and growthful experiences, having strongly positive affective components and playing a dominant role in the genesis of personality resources, and thus significantly affecting personality development.' He hypothesizes that such experiences have a great deal to do with human growth, development, and potentialities.

Our humanistic researcher, let us say, is struck by the similarity between Otto's hypothesis and the claims of drama specialists about how drama helps children grow. His interest is heightened by the discovery that the sensory awareness exercises used in drama resemble the group methods used by Otto. Minerva participants, for example, are asked to recall and describe, in free-associative form, a particular sensation, which typically sets off a new series of personal recollections: 'The description of odours (an appeal to one of the most primitive and basic senses) at times produces a flow of memories and associations and can be used a number of times repeatedly' (Otto). Drama students are asked to use their senses to stimulate imagination and develop concentration: 'Be aware of and enjoy smells that you yourself find particularly pleasant; let these smells evoke imaginative circumstances; let different smells evoke memories from the past; remember clearly' (Brian Way). The immediate purposes of the two activities are admittedly different, but do they not arise out of the same experiential matrix, and is not the apparent connection between them worth exploring?

The humanistic researcher, then, becomes interested in investigating the phenomenon of heightened experiences in drama: How often do they occur? How intensely are they felt? Is their effect always positive? Having formulated the problem, he sets out to discover all he can about it.

His first resource is himself: What have been his own experiences with heightened states of consciousness? He recalls instances of personal rapture and transport, searching for pattern and meaning in the inward flow of his associations and memories. When he has reached the limits of his own intuitive vision and comprehension and has formed some tentative impressions, he sets out to investigate experientially.

He finds a drama class or workshop and immerses himself in it. He participates in its activities, observes their effects on students, discusses his impressions with the teacher. He becomes as receptive as he can to the whole of his experience, while organizing his perception around the problem at hand. He steps back from time to time to review what has happened, interviewing participants, studying tapes and transcripts, and refining his initial impressions accordingly.

At last he begins to discern intelligible patterns of relationships. As the patterns crystallize, the researcher can conceptualize them in clearer terms, and after a time he has enough evidence to convince him that such relationships actually exist. He has reference to other research and theories to check and clarify his formulations. He then presents a set of hypotheses of the sort: Heightened experiences occur more often in certain identifiable types of students than in others, because of certain theoretically important differences in their needs or cognitive styles or linguistic backgrounds or whatever. These are his 'discoveries,' which are, of course, subject to verification. Hypotheses based on experiential knowledge may often be amenable to more rigorous investigative procedures. But presently that concern is secondary to the need for close, thorough, sensitive probing into the nature of drama. That, I think, is our fundamental task.

REFERENCES

JOURARD, Sidney. (1968). *Disclosing Man to Himself*. Princeton, N.J.: Van Nostrand.

MASLOW, Abraham. (1970). *Motivation and Personality*. 2nd ed. New York: Harper and Row.

MASLOW, Abraham (1966). *The Psychology of Science*. New York: Harper and Row.

MOUSTAKAS, Clark (1961). *Loneliness*. Englewood Cliffs, N.J.: Prentice-Hall.

ORNSTEIN, Robert (1973). *The Psychology of Consciousness*. New York: Viking Press.

OTTO, Herbert A. (1967). 'The Minerva Experience: Initial Report.' In: BUGENTAL, James F.T. (ed.) *Challenges of Humanistic Psychology*. New York: McGraw-Hill.

POLANYI, Michael (1958). *Personal Knowledge*. University of Chicago Press.

SEVERIN, Frank T. (1965). *Humanistic Viewpoints in Psychology*. New York: McGraw-Hill.

WAY, Brian (1967). *Development through Drama*. New York: Humanities Press.

WEIL, Andrew (1972). *The Natural Mind*. Boston: Houghton Mifflin.